EAT TH
SPEAK T

"Acts13:1 tells us that the mark of the Apostolic missionary sending church at Antioch was that 'there were Prophets and Teachers there.' A healthy and fruitful church and individual Christian must embrace both the teacher and the prophet. Disaster comes when we divide the two and opt for one over the other. Rachel Hickson is widely acknowledged as both a prophet and a teacher. In her latest book, she boils down years of mature experience to offer us a balanced, biblical, pastoral, practical and often inspirational handbook on how to grow in handling both the 'taught' and the 'caught' Word of God. This is a real gem at a time when there is much muddled thinking on these matters."

– **Simon Ponsonby,** *Pastor of Theology, St Aldates, Oxford*

"In *Eat the Word, Speak the Word,* Rachel highlights a vital principle for prophetic ministry: before bringing a 'now word' from God by the Spirit, we need to be building our lives on the 'eternal Word', the Bible. Her first three chapters lay an excellent foundation for the rest of the book, reminding us that on a very regular basis we need to allow God to speak to us through His Word, by His Spirit. Then and only then can we safely, powerfully and consistently be trusted with the wonderful gift of prophecy and prophetic ministry. This honouring of Word and Spirit is something that Rachel demonstrates both in her ministry and her writings. I commend this book to you: read and be inspired!"

– **Dr David Smith,** *Senior Leader, KingsGate Community Church, Peterborough*

"This is Rachel at her best. Some people think negatively with regard to the term 'balanced' ministry but one of the highest accolades I could offer is to say that this book is a wisely balanced book. It is helpful for an individual who wants to move in the prophetic. It is helpful for church leaders who are consistently looking for authentic prophetic ministry to support the development of a church. It is also helpful beyond local churches as we grapple to understand the bigger picture of what God is doing in our nation and beyond.

"Any book that connects 'Spirit' and 'Word' automatically gets my attention as I personally believe that the Holy Spirit is emphasizing this connection in today's church. Rachel rightly takes us back to the Bible as the starting point for all prophetic ministry and challenges us with regard to our love for and knowledge of God's Word. It's great that within the same book there is teaching on 'Apostolic and Prophetic foundations' and teaching on 'How to put together a local church prayer team'. This book gives access points into the prophetic for everyone. Highly recommended!"

– **Stuart Bell,** *Senior Pastor of New Life Christian Fellowship, Lincoln, and Leader of the Ground Level network of churches*

EAT THE WORD
SPEAK THE WORD

RACHEL HICKSON

MONARCH
BOOKS

Oxford, UK & Grand Rapids, Michigan, USA

First published in the UK in 2010 by Monarch Books
(a publishing imprint of Lion Hudson plc)
Wilkinson House, Jordan Hill Road, Oxford OX2 8DR, England
Tel: +44 (0)1865 302750 Fax: +44 (0)1865 302757
Email: monarch@lionhudson.com
www.lionhudson.com

Reprinted 2010.

ISBN 978 1 85424 971 5 (UK)

Distributed by:
UK: Marston Book Services, PO Box 269, Abingdon, Oxon, OX14 4YN
USA: Kregel Publications, PO Box 2607, Grand Rapids, Michigan 49501

Contents

I DEDICATE THIS BOOK TO MY DAD,
ALAN VINCENT.

YOU HAVE BEEN AN INSPIRATION TO ME AND TAUGHT
ME HOW TO RESPECT, LOVE AND TEACH THE BIBLE.

THANK YOU FOR "INFECTING" ME WITH A PASSION
FOR JESUS AND SHOWING ME A LIFE THAT BLENDS THE
WORD AND THE SPIRIT.

Acknowledgments

This part of the book is impossible to write! How can you express your gratitude to each person who deserves it? I am sure I will forget someone – so thanks to all of you!

But as always I do want to thank my husband, Gordon, for releasing me to write, especially over these summer months. You are great and such an encouragement to me!

I also want to thank Tony Collins and the team at Monarch for their easy yet professional manner as we have worked together on this book. It has been a joy to work with you – thank you!

I also want to thank an army of volunteers who have read the manuscript, helped correct my grammar and given me hope. Thank you for all your reading time!

Finally, thank *you* for buying this book. I hope that it will be more than just another book and that it will stir in you a deep hunger for God and his Word.

So now *enjoy*!

Introduction

When I was a child my father taught me to love the Word of God, and his love for the Bible was contagious. The Bible he read seemed to be different from my Bible, and he had such an amazing way of digging into the truths of each phrase and fascinating me with his insights. His understanding and appreciation of his Bible made me hungry for more.

In this book I want to explore the prophetic ministry from the perspective of first having a deep love for the Word of God. As a minister I have discovered the power of the spoken word to change lives and I have seen the effect of both the prophetic and the preached word to open revelation for people's lives. Unfortunately, I have also seen poor prophetic ministry that has not been firmly rooted in the Bible causing chaos. So we need to be balanced prophets who eat the Word and then speak the Word!

This book will take you, the reader, on a journey that will teach you to respect and handle the Word of God correctly and then train the prophetic gift within you. I believe that it is time for every believer to have a new love affair with the Word of God. We all have seasons when we struggle to read our Bibles, and if we are not careful, this can stir a wrong fascination for the prophetic ministry, and we become prophet-hunters rather than God-chasers. But God has a

Word for each of us today and we need to have a fresh desire and discipline to eat this Word.

But also in this season of history, our nations also have a lack of knowledge and understanding concerning the Word of God, and we need the prophet's cry. We need a prophetic people to arise with a strong, clear sound: "This is the Word of the Lord!" We need to clearly hear what the Spirit is saying to the churches, as most of us desire to only do what the Holy Spirit is telling us to do! This is the time for the mature prophetic gift to speak out. So as we hunger for the Word, and give ourselves to the place of intimacy and prayer, God will speak to us and we will become an intelligent army who are doing the right thing, at the right time, in the right place! This book seeks to inspire you to read your Bible more deeply, speak God's Word more profoundly, and understand his revelation more completely. It is time for us to arise, to *eat* his word and to *speak* his Word, and then to watch as nations change, people are restored, and churches grow, as his Word reveals its power.

CHAPTER 1

The Bible – What a Treasure!

I was standing in a room alive with expectation. Every eye was fixed on me and every word I spoke was grasped with eager excitement. This was China. Seated in front of me, on narrow benches, was a group of 250 people of all ages, but predominantly women. They were squeezed into a dilapidated farmhouse room. They were hungry for the Word of God. As I began to speak I noticed their attentiveness. I had been asked to speak from sunrise to sunset, allowing just three short breaks for food, so this was the first session at 5 a.m. I had been warned that most Western preachers were not able to take the pace over five days, so some Chinese pastors were ready to take my place when I became too tired to speak about Jesus. The pastor informed me that these farming people had gathered here because God had sent them: they did not advertise or announce these meetings, but these people had come to this farmhouse led by the Holy Spirit, hungry for the Word of God, and it was our responsibility to feed them! I thought about this miracle, as the farmhouse was in the middle of the rice-fields, miles away from any roads or major city. (We had driven for four hours from Shanghai, then hidden in the back of a tractor trailer for one and a half hours, and finally walked for forty-five minutes to find this place.) So now I had the privilege to speak the Word in China.

As I opened my Bible I watched these faces stream with tears, and then when I referred to a particular scripture, suddenly an unscripted scene unfolded in front of me. Immediately about ten of these people, who had been seated so still in front of me, shot to their feet and, at the top of their voices, recited something in Chinese, and then promptly sat down and resumed their attentive position. This scene repeated itself every time I quoted a Bible reference. Finally my translator explained to me that the Chinese love their Bible and they consider it their greatest joy to be able to quote Scripture, so whenever I announced a Bible reference, they would stand to read it or recite it from memory so that they could have the privilege of speaking God's Word. This continued over the next five days, and I left this farmhouse with a new sense of honour and reverence for the Bible that I once held so casually in my hands. This book is the Word of God, and what an incredible treasure it is! The Bible is the most amazing book, but do I love it, value it and eat it enough?

WHAT'S IN A WORD?

So what is this book called the Bible? Many of us have numerous copies at home, in different translations, but this book is like no other book. It is unique and powerful, and just its physical presence stirs up trouble! No book has ever had the popularity or notoriety that the Bible has had. No book has ever sold as many copies. It has consistently topped the best-seller list since its first publication. Rarely ever mentioned in these lists, the Bible sells over 44 million copies a year worldwide and well over a million in the UK alone. An article in *The Times* newspaper commented on this:

> Forget the modern British novelist and television tie-ins: the Bible is the biggest-selling book every year. If cumulative sales of the Bible were frankly reflected in bestseller lists, it would be a rare week when anything else got a look-in. Is it wonderful, weird, or just plain baffling in this increasingly godless age, when the range of books available grows wider with each passing year, that this one book should go on selling hand over fist, month in, month out? It's estimated that nearly 1¼ million Bibles and Testaments are sold in the UK each year.[1]

The Bible is also one of the few books throughout history to have been repeatedly banned or burned by governments and regimes because of its dangerous and subversive content! The Catholic News Agency reported on 2 November 2007 that:

> Organizers of the 2008 Olympics in Beijing have published a list of "prohibited objects" in the Olympic village where athletes will stay. To the surprise of many, Bibles are among the objects that will not be allowed. According to the Italian daily *La Gazzetta dello Sport*, organizers have cited "security reasons" and have prohibited athletes from bearing any kind of religious symbol at Olympic facilities.

So the Bible is popular, and some people see it as a threat – but is it your treasure? Do you love this Word? At the coronation of our British Queen, she was handed a copy of the Bible by the Moderator of the General Assembly of the Church of Scotland. As he handed her the Bible, he said this: "We present you with this book, the most valuable thing that this world affords."

WE NEED FRESH BREAD

As I walked into the grocery store the aroma of fresh bread hit my senses, and suddenly bread was at the top of my shopping list and I was hungry. The smell of freshly baked bread has a remarkable ability to immediately stimulate hunger! In the same way, we must ask God to awaken this desire in us for his Word, the Bible. Many of us have an appetite for the prophetic word in our lives, considering this experience more powerful or exciting. But I believe we must be balanced lovers of both the Bible and the prophetic word if we are to be sane Christians. If we want to be safe prophets, we must value the Bible as our greatest treasure!

> *Jesus answered, "It is written: 'Man does not live on bread alone, but on every word that comes from the mouth of God.'"*
>
> Matthew 4:4

We see this appetite throughout history. People needed the Word of God in their lives. Initially the Word of God was passed down from generation to generation in an oral form. This was sufficient for many years. But the time came when people yearned for their own Bible in a written form, and since then possessing a copy of the Bible has been the goal and desire of millions of men and women from every nation and background. Throughout history people have gone to great lengths to obtain a Bible, and heroes have risked their lives to open the way for their generation to read for themselves the Word of God in their own language.

MARY JONES AND HER BIBLE

I wonder if you can remember your first significant encounter with the Bible? I remember when I was ten years old, sitting on my bed one Sunday afternoon during the quiet time at boarding school, and suddenly becoming fascinated with my Bible. I had just signed up for a Bible competition in which I had to read the Bible in six months and write out my favourite verse from each chapter in a notebook. I was reading the New Testament first, and suddenly the Gospels captivated me and the love of Jesus for people challenged me. I began to cry and God stirred in me a deep new love for this book.

Throughout history we read of an army of ordinary people who became desperate for a Bible. Here is the story of Mary Jones and her Bible. I remember this story being read to me while I was still at school. I was so touched that a young girl had to sacrifice so much because she wanted a Bible, and it caused me to look at mine with a new respect.

Mary Jones was from a poor family, the daughter of a weaver who lived at the foot of Cader Idris, in Llanfihangel-y-pennant, Wales. She was born in December 1784. Her parents were Methodists and Mary made her own decision to follow Jesus at eight years of age. Having learned to read, Mary began to have a burning desire to possess a Bible of her own. After some investigation she discovered that the nearest copy of the Bible was available at a farm two miles away from her little cottage, but there was no copy for sale nearer than

Bala, a further twenty-five miles away. Welsh Bibles were scarce in those days and too expensive for most ordinary people to afford. But Mary decided to take on as many jobs as she could and she saved for six years until she had enough money to pay for her own copy. She started one morning in 1800 (now aged 16) for Bala, and walked the twenty-five miles, barefoot as usual, to obtain a copy from the Revd Charles, the only individual with Bibles for sale in the area. According to one version of the story, Mr Charles told her that all of the copies which he had received were sold or already spoken for. Mary was so distraught that he spared her one of the copies already promised to another.

Mary died at the age of eighty-two. In the town of Llanfihangel, a monument has been erected with the following inscription in both English and Welsh:

> To the remembrance of Mary Jones, who in 1800 at the age of 16, walked from here to Bala, in order to buy a Bible from Rev. Charles in the Welsh language. This event was the cause of the foundation of the British and Foreign Bible Society.

Mary's copy of the Bible still survives and, inscribed in her own hand in English on the last page of the Apocrypha, are these words (the spelling is her own):

> Mary Jones was born 16th of December 1784. I bought this in the 16th year of my age. I am Daughter of Jacob Jones and Mary Jones His wife. The Lord may give me grace. Amen. Mary Jones His [is] The True Onour [owner] of this Bible. Bought In the Year 1800, Aged 16th.

Take a moment to consider your Bible and ask God to give you a new hunger and sense of privilege for your Bible. In today's society we are often totally unaware of the journey that many have made so that we can possess a Bible. We have grown so familiar with our access to a Bible that we do not understand or even know about the struggle and price that many endured so that we can have a Bible in our own language today. So, let us take a look at history, follow in the footsteps of martyrs, and trace the story of our English Bible.

THE JOURNEY OF THE BIBLE IN EUROPE: JOHN WYCLIFFE TO MARTIN LUTHER

In England, making the Word of God available to the common man in English was a privilege fought and paid for with people's lives. The institutional church was threatened by this action, as it meant they would no longer control access to the Scriptures. The church feared that if people were able to read the Bible in their own tongue, its income and power would crumble. They would not be able to continue to get away with selling indulgences (the forgiveness of sins) or selling the release of loved ones from a church-manufactured "Purgatory". People would begin to challenge the church's authority as its leaders were exposed as frauds and thieves. The contradictions between what God's Word said, and what the priests taught, would be open to the public's eyes and the truth would set them free from the grip of fear that the institutional church held. Salvation through faith, not works or donations, would be able to be understood.

Against this turbulent background, the first handwritten English-language Bible manuscripts were produced in the

1380s by John Wycliffe, an Oxford professor, scholar and theologian. Wycliffe was well known throughout Europe for his opposition to the teaching of the organized church, which he believed to be contrary to the Bible. With the help of his followers, called the Lollards, Wycliffe produced dozens of English-language copies of the Scriptures. They were translated out of the Latin Vulgate, which was the only source text available to Wycliffe. The Pope was so infuriated by his teachings and his translation of the Bible into English that forty-four years after Wycliffe died, he ordered the scholar's bones to be dug up, crushed and scattered in a river!

One of Wycliffe's followers, John Hus, actively promoted Wycliffe's belief that people should be permitted to read the Bible in their own language. Hus was burned at the stake in 1415; Wycliffe's manuscript Bibles were used as kindling for the fire! The last words of John Hus were: "In 100 years, God will raise up a man whose calls for reform cannot be suppressed." Almost exactly 100 years later, in 1517, Martin Luther nailed his famous 95 Theses of Contention (a list of the Roman Catholic Church's crimes and heretical doctrines) onto the church door at Wittenberg. The prophecy of Hus had come true. Martin Luther went on to be the first man to print the Bible in the German language. Foxe's *Book of Martyrs* records that in that same year, 1517, seven people were burned at the stake for the crime of teaching their children to say the Lord's Prayer in English rather than Latin.

In the 1490s Thomas Linacre (another Oxford professor and the personal physician to Kings Henry VII and Henry VIII) decided to learn Greek. After reading the Gospels in Greek, and comparing it to the Latin Vulgate, he wrote in his diary: "Either this [the original Greek] is not the Gospel… or we are not Christians." The Latin had become so corrupt that it no longer even preserved the message of the Gospel, yet the church still threatened to kill anyone who read the Scriptures in any language other than Latin, even though Latin was not an original language of the Scriptures.

In 1496, John Colet, yet another Oxford professor and the son of the Mayor of London, started reading the New Testament in Greek and translating it into English for his students at Oxford, and later for the public at St Paul's Cathedral in London. The people were so hungry to hear the Word of God in a language they could understand that within six months there were 20,000 people packed into the church and at least that many outside trying to get in! Fortunately for Colet, he was a powerful man with friends in high places, so, amazingly, he managed to avoid execution.[2]

Wycliffe's legacy survived and inspired the creation of Wycliffe Bible Translators who, to this day, work to bring the Word of God to every tribe in their native tongue. So we have reaped where others have sown in sacrifice and even with their lives. We are privileged to have a Bible in our own language. So each time we pick up our Bible, let us carry it with a new sense of gratitude for those who have left us this legacy of the Word of God in our language. This actual printed copy of the Bible, that we can treat so familiarly, is the fruit of a fierce battle that brave men and women fought in order to ensure that we can hold our own copy today. It is time to explore and appreciate this treasure more fully! Even if we have previously struggled to spend time reading the Bible when we are alone, I believe that God wants to stir a new ability to read and love this book. So, get ready for a fresh impartation as, in the next chapter, we will explore how we can read our Bibles with a new passion and discipline, and enjoy it!

Notes

1. *The Times*, 1996. See also "Bible boom in the Credit Crunch", *The Times*, March 20 2009
2. http://www.greatsite.com/timeline-english-bible-history/

CHAPTER 2

Reading the Bible and Loving It

Anyone who has been a Christian for a few years will have heard preachers encouraging them to make sure they read their Bible the whole way through and that they continue to do so regularly. This can be a source of guilt for those who haven't read the whole Bible and who find the prospect daunting. But I believe we need not be overawed by the thought of reading the Bible cover to cover, if we put the task into perspective.

I believe that as we walk with him, God wants to teach us how to take hold of his Word and establish a strong grasp on it in our lives, so that we learn to love his Word and grow in our confidence in handling it. His desire is to remove the intimidation of the enemy who accuses us, saying, "You're a lousy Christian because I know you don't read the Word. You don't know what it says!" If we can stop being intimidated and get past the barrier of being afraid to handle the Word confidently, then I believe that so much of what the Bible says about God's Word dwelling in us richly will be true for us.

I read this wonderful quote by Dwight L. Moody: "The Scriptures were not given to increase our knowledge, but to change our lives." It is so important that we grasp this fundamental principle. Reading the Bible is not meant to be an intellectual battle, where we grapple with it and try to fathom its meaning with our minds. We have to grasp the Word by faith, believing that it has the power to transform us from the inside out. The purpose of the Word is to change us, not to help us earn a degree. We should not be reading the Bible in order to gain a lot of head knowledge. Instead, as we read, it is our spirits (usually without us even realizing it) that are being affected.

The Word needs to be the bedrock of our lives and the place where our feet are planted so that we are stable, secure and immovable in our faith. A while ago God showed me a picture of a person who was standing on a small foundation stone. It was firm and solid, just not very big. God asked me, "Rachel, what happens when someone comes to intimidate you and gets right in your face?" The answer, of course, is you step back. The point is: if you are only standing on something one metre square, then when the enemy comes to intimidate you, you are going to fall off!

Instead, our lives need to be based on a broad, firm foundation, where no matter what intimidation is thrown at us, we will not fall off. That comes from having a real, deep knowledge of God's Word. When the enemy comes and intimidates us, saying, "You're nothing, you're worthless, you're a failure," we need to be standing on a solid foundation and have God's Word inside of us. Then we can respond, "No, I am fearfully and wonderfully made; God has loved me from the day of my conception; he works all things together for my good; he is with me, he will never forsake me; he will never leave me; I am altogether beautiful; he has called me…" The Word gives us knowledge of the truth, and we need to know the truth about ourselves in Christ in order to defeat the enemy's attacks.

GOD-BREATHED

2 Timothy 3:16 says:

All Scripture is God-breathed and is useful for teaching, rebuking, correcting and training in righteousness, so that the man of God may be thoroughly equipped for every good work.

I love that scripture. That's what the Word of God is to us: the breath of God. As we read the Bible there is breath in it; it is so much more than simply the printed word. As we read, the Holy Spirit can lift the very words off the page and breathe them into us.

Do you remember the old Xerox photocopier advert which showed a stream of words flying through the air, being blown around by the wind? The words eventually floated down from the sky and got themselves into the correct order and we could then understand what they were saying. This is how I picture reading the Bible. The Holy Spirit picks up a jumble of words and blows them off the page into our spirit, ordering them so that they have an impact on us. He literally writes the words on our heart.

The devil would like us to believe that reading the Bible is a waste of time and doesn't accomplish anything, but this is not true. Something supernatural happens as we read because we have taken the time to hear from God and God has taken the time to communicate with us. Paul told Timothy that the God-inspired Scriptures were useful for teaching us, rebuking us, correcting us and training us. We have to let the Word work in our life in this way if we want to be prepared and equipped to go out and do valuable work for God.

Picture yourself holding your Bible up in one hand,

gripping it with your four fingers and thumb. Someone once suggested that there are five ways of reading your Bible, each one represented by your fingers and thumb. I find this a very easy way of reminding myself of the variety of ways in which we can interact with God's Word. This is important because I believe that in order to get the most out of our Bibles, we need a strategy of variety. Otherwise reading our Bibles will become a chore.

It's good, therefore, to understand that when we spend time in the Word there are a number of different ways to "grip" it. The five different methods we can use for personal study are:

1. Hearing
2. Reading
3. Studying
4. Memorizing
5. Meditating

1. HEAR THE WORD

Throughout this chapter I'm going to quote a lot of Scripture because Scripture teaches best. God's Word is both incredibly down to earth and highly relevant. I love the Bible because it never dates. I also love it because it is a powerful tool in our hands.

In Judges chapter 6 we read the story of Gideon. Gideon is complaining to God, saying:

Where are all the signs and wonders that our fathers used to tell us about? Where is the revival? Why, if You are with us, is all this happening around us in our community? Why are we living in such a barren and

God-forsaken land? If You are for us, explain to me,
God, why all these things are happening.

Judges 6:13–14 (my paraphrase)

God answers Gideon's questions:

Then the Lord turned to him and said, "Go with
the strength you have, and rescue Israel from the
Midianites. I am sending you!"

Judges 6:13–14 NLT

What God says, in effect, is: "I know what you're looking at, Gideon. You can see everything going terribly wrong, but actually the answer is in your own hand."

The same is true for us today. We often become consumed by our problems and the circumstances around us, and yet we are holding the solution in our hands. The answers we are looking for are in the Word of God and we have the Word in our hands. It is already with us – we just have to hear it and believe it. Romans 10:17 says:

Consequently, faith comes from hearing the message,
and the message is heard through the word of Christ.

Isn't that interesting? If you feel that you are struggling to have faith in your life, what do you need? You need to do a bit more hearing of God's Word, because it will result in faith. Faith comes from hearing the Word of Christ.

How can we *hear* the Word? These days we are literally spoilt for choice. We can hear in many different ways. You can hear the Word on tapes, CDs, via the radio and television, or in songs. Some worship CDs are literally the Word in song, psalms with accompaniment. All these are valid ways of getting the Word into you. Even listening to the Bible on CD, as opposed to someone's sermons, is incredibly beneficial and gives a different appreciation of the Word.

Hearing the Bible takes place on two levels. We can hear it with our natural ears, but also with our "spiritual ears" – that is, in our heart. Hearing naturally, we might say, "Oh, that's interesting. I'd forgotten that bit..." This is a perfectly valid way of hearing. So often we set high expectations on ourselves and want to receive an earth-shattering revelation every time we pick up the Bible. Instead we can relax and just enjoy hearing the story. The Bible *is* God's story. The text hasn't always got a profound, hidden meaning. Part of it is just God telling us his story. But when we hear with our spiritual ears, we hear God's Spirit speaking behind the story, and the words come alive in our spirit.

Luke 8:15 says:

But the seed on good soil stands for those with a noble and good heart, who hear the word, retain it, and by persevering produce a crop.

We know that the seed in this parable represents the Word of God because Jesus says, "The seed is the Word of God." So we could say, "The Word of God on good soil stands for those with a noble and good heart..."

In order to hear the Bible clearly with our spiritual ears, we need to cultivate good soil for the seed of the Word to be planted into. Then, Jesus tells us, we will be able to retain it, persevere with it and produce a good crop in our life. In other words, we will receive all the spiritual benefit from it that God intends. What is this "good soil"? It is our heart. We need to have an open and prepared heart to hear and receive God's Word.

I believe this is one of the main reasons why God has taken issue with unforgiveness in the church and his Spirit has addressed it so strongly. Nothing messes up our hearts more than unforgiveness. It is like spiritual cholesterol – it blocks up the heart and makes us sick. If we get rid of every shred of unforgiveness, it brings healing to our hearts and we can begin to hear the Word clearly, retain it, persevere with it and produce a harvest from it. If we really want to hear and benefit from God's Word, we have to let the Holy Spirit rebuke and correct us. As he deals with our hearts we are able to grow in our love for the Word.

Nehemiah 8:8 says:

They read from the Book of the Law of God, making it clear and giving the meaning so that the people could understand what was being read.

1 Timothy 4:13 says:

Until I come, devote yourself to the public reading of Scripture, to preaching and to teaching.

There is something special about the Word of God being read aloud in public and I believe we should make more space for it in our churches. We often assume that everyone who comes to church knows all the Bible stories, but guess what? They don't! It's good to publicly read the stories, the parables, the Scriptures, just as they used to in the Old Testament.

Nehemiah 8:8 tells us that the purpose of the reading was to make God's Word clear and tell people what it meant so they could understand it. This is why it is valid and important for us to have conferences where the Bible is taught by a variety of teachers.

Occasionally you will hear someone teaching from the Bible and think, "Oh, I've never heard that verse explained in that way before, but it really makes sense to me." Often the same truths expressed in a different style, with a slightly different emphasis, will really connect with us because we hear them afresh. If we only ever listen to the same person preaching over and over again, we are in danger of boxing ourselves in spiritually and becoming biased. A varied diet is much better!

My observation, particularly in the British church, is that we are not very good at taking notes when we listen to others teaching the Word, but this is a good discipline to acquire. Rather than hearing the Word and hoping we will retain it, it is far better to take notes. If we value the Word, then we should do something to help ourselves retain it so that we can then persevere with it in order to be fruitful. We can review our notes in our private times and ask God to help us to apply the Word to our life.

Listening to the Word should then inspire us to go on to read and study it more.

2. READ THE WORD

There is a clear distinction between reading the Word and studying it that will become apparent as you read on, but they are closely linked, and most of us will mix the two together. They are, however, separate skills, each of which needs to be honed.

There was a time when I got into deep study: I examined the meaning of every single word and each word itself opened up a whole new horizon of study. This kind of intense interaction can be quite tiring and time consuming, and there are seasons in life when we haven't got time to study in this way. I used to be a disciplined student until I had two children! I had a baby boy for whom sleep seemed to be of no importance! So every time the house was peaceful I just wanted to sleep, never mind study. If you are in that position, you shouldn't feel guilty about it, because it's just a season of life. Instead we can make a bit of time to simply read.

It's amazing what you can imbibe even if you are only reading something casually. If you read it, it tends to go in. Advertisers have learnt this. Why else would they put up so many advertisements on billboards or in magazines? We all know that we can take in information as we drive by a billboard on our way to drop the kids off at school, without even properly reading the ad! It's the same with the Bible. We can just read it, and it still does its work.

Reading is about getting to know the stories and the characters in the Bible. Some people feel that the Old Testament is not as relevant as the New Testament in today's society, so why should we read both? I believe both are equally valid and essential if we want a complete understanding of our God. The way I approach this is as follows. God reveals different aspects of his character and personality in each of the biblical books. In the Old Testament we see the face of judgment and law and in the New Testament we read more about the gifts of grace and forgiveness. Obviously there are some aspects of God's character and person which we only appreciate fully after Christ comes. So while both Testaments talk about the same God, each one is distinctive in the way it introduces us to His character and personality.

It's helpful to think in terms of the difference that takes place in a person before and after marriage. In covenant language, Rachel Vincent was the old covenant and Rachel Hickson is the new covenant. A new covenant was made in my life on 21 March 1981. On that day, I stood in front of a congregation and said, "I take thee, Gordon Crawford Fitzgerald Hickson [how did I remember all those names?!] as my lawfully wedded husband." From that moment, my name changed and so did my covenant status. Did I suddenly change my whole personality? No. Everything I was up until that point as Rachel Vincent did not disappear. But having married Gordon, the two of us became one, and different areas of my nature were revealed as Rachel Hickson that could not be revealed as Rachel Vincent. The different "faces" of my personality have changed because the relationship has changed.

It's the same with God. God has not suddenly cut off a section of his personality because he has introduced a new covenant. The God of Genesis is the God of Revelation – exactly the same. But because Jesus hung on the cross and died, and the Old Covenant was superseded by the New Covenant, we can now see a whole other face of our wonderful God. This has been revealed because of the cross and because of his grace. It does not mean that the God of the Old Testament does not exist any more. That is still part of who he is.

This is why I believe we must read the whole Bible from Genesis to Revelation, because then we see the full spectrum of the glory of all that God is. We all have our favourite books because they represent facets of God's character that we relate to the most. But if we don't explore the full book, we don't explore the full character of God. You have to read it from cover to cover. Revelation 1:3 says:

> Blessed is the one who reads the words of this prophecy...

I was challenged by this verse when I read it recently, because it had been a long time since I'd read Revelation. To tell you the truth, even though I am a prophetic person, it is one book that I struggle to read as a whole. I have favourite verses in it, but I find it difficult to read. The verse continues:

... and blessed are those who hear it and take to heart what is written in it, because the time is near.

Do you want to receive a blessing? Then read the book of Revelation. That's what the Bible says.

I have found it helpful in my devotional times to read aloud occasionally. This is a useful discipline, especially if you are feeling a bit depressed or oppressed, because declaring the Word verbally does something to break that. Reading aloud can also give verses a different emphasis and help us to understand them in a new light. As we read out extensive passages it begins to become more like a novel than a reference book. We understand the story that is being told, not just the information.

Sometimes it's good to have a Bible translation purely for reading and a separate one for studying. There is always a debate about which version is the best. Should we read the NIV, the NKJV, the RSV or the NLT? I think what you are doing, reading or studying should determine which version you use. Sometimes you want an easy read; at other times you need a more study/reference-orientated version to work from. Pick a version that suits you, which you can understand and relate to. Usually it is a good thing to refer to a variety of translations or to change your main version from time to time, because it helps you to gain a more balanced perspective on what the Scriptures are teaching.

3. STUDY THE WORD

There are lots of scriptures in the Bible about studying the Word. One of my favourites is Acts 17:11, which says:

> Now the Bereans were of more noble character than the Thessalonians, for they received the message with great eagerness and examined the Scriptures every day to see if what Paul said was true.

This group of people, the Bereans, had heard the message of the gospel from Paul and it sparked an interest in them to go and study it. Rather than simply taking his word for it, these people studied the Scriptures "every day" in order to establish that what Paul was saying was true.

When you hear a preacher speaking about a new idea that you've not heard before, it is a good idea to go home and check it out. Study the Scriptures, dig through them, and understand them in their context. See if you can go along 100 per cent with what was said. You have to examine the Word to see that it is true. If you hear an interesting concept, it is worth looking it up to see if it is repeated anywhere else in the Bible.

Both the reading and the hearing of the Word should stir us to want to go deeper. Studying the Bible is digging into its fullest depths. Look into the background of verses, look into the meaning of words, look into their applications, and look into some of the culture. All these things will help us to better understand what is being said.

Culture, in particular, is important for Christians in the West to understand because the context of the Bible is not our own. If you understand something of the culture of biblical times, then your perspective on the text will change dramatically.

One example of this that impacted me was studying what it meant to reach the age of thirty in Jewish culture. Thirty was a very significant birthday. Luke chapter 3 recounts how, when Jesus was thirty years old, he sought out John the Baptist in the wilderness in order to be baptized. As he was baptized, God the Father spoke from heaven saying, "You are my Son, whom I love; with you I am well pleased…"

You could think, that's wonderful – end of story. But understanding the cultural implications of what is happening here makes the story so much more powerful. The thirtieth birthday of a son in Jewish culture marked a time of transition, a baton change. It was the time when a father would hand over the running of the family business to his son and throw a huge party. People of significance would be invited – prominent business people, the equivalent of the local mayor, other dignitaries – and they would go to the father's house to celebrate his son's thirtieth birthday. They would kill a fatted calf, spread the table with food and drink, and then in the middle of the party the father would stand up and point to his son and say in front of everyone, "This is my beloved son in whom I have placed my favour."

Normally it would be the firstborn son of the family, but actually the father had a choice. He could choose a different son if he wanted to, or even choose to adopt a son of the village to inherit his business. This was much more than the father simply saying, "I'm really pleased with you – well done, boy!" What the father was really saying was, "I am placing the favour of inheritance upon you. I'm giving you the keys. From now on, the business, the bank accounts and all the finances – they're all yours."

What a difference this makes to our understanding of Jesus' baptism in the wilderness! Here Jesus comes on his thirtieth birthday. He comes to his Father's house and steps into the water. He is being baptized and suddenly *boom*! God the Father speaks: "This is my beloved Son…" Jesus is officially inaugurated into the family business and from that moment on, he carries as much authority as the Father.

The word for "son" which is used is the Greek *huios*. There are five different words for "son" used in the Greek biblical text. They have various meanings (*tekno*, for instance, means "a small child"), but *huios* refers to a mature son, someone who has reached thirty years of age and has therefore gained the rights of inheritance. This is what makes Paul's words, directed at us, in Galatians 3:26 so amazing:

> You are all sons [huios] of God through faith in Christ
> Jesus.

Paul deliberately used the word *huios* to demonstrate that in Christ we are recognized as mature sons and daughters of God, adopted by him and chosen to receive an inheritance. God is saying, "I am giving you the full rights of inheritance to everything I own in heaven."

This is why it is worth studying the Word! We don't receive these kinds of insights when we are simply reading.

There are many books you can use to help you study: Bible dictionaries, atlases, commentaries, concordances, topical references, and just listening to good preachers. There are also many superb Bible computer packages these days. You don't have to fill your library with hundreds of books that cost you a fortune. If you've got a reasonable computer you can buy some software which is a lot cheaper than buying all the books.

Bible PC packages have two main approaches, and you have to decide the way you like to study. Some of them take the view that you are sitting in the middle of a library with an expert librarian. You say, "I need to know this" and the librarian fetches you a range of books that are relevant to your question. All sorts of references and concordances are opened up and you can then sift through the information that interests you. Personally, I prefer this approach.

The second approach, which is more appropriate for those who are serious students, or who have a background of theological training, takes the view that you are sitting in the middle of the library and lets you choose which books you want to look at and interrogate. The "librarian" in this case simply tells you which books are available and it is down to you to determine which ones will help you in your study. So, you have to ask yourself the question, "How do I like to work? Which will be best for me?"

Proverbs 2:1–5 says:

My son, if you accept my words
and store up my commands within you,
turning your ear to wisdom
and applying your heart to understanding,
and if you call out for insight
and cry aloud for understanding,
and if you look for it as for silver
and search for it as for hidden treasure,
then you will understand the fear of the Lord
and find the knowledge of God.

These verses present us with a wonderful picture of what it means to study the Word. If we go digging in the Word we will always strike gold, so we need to go on a treasure hunt! Study can sometimes be difficult, but the effort will always be worth it in the end.

Sometimes reading the Word of God can be like eating a fish that contains a lot of bones. I remember my mother always had this thing about kippers. I never did, because I hated picking through all the bones. Nevertheless, Mum always used to try to convince me that there was some good fish there. I remember God said to me one day, "Rachel, you read the Bible like that. You just notice the bones. You focus on the things you can't understand and let them choke you. But you have read many other things which have blessed you. Concentrate on the things that bless you and push the bones to one side."

This was a revelation to me. I realized that there comes a time when you can go back and address the more difficult things in the Bible as you grow in maturity. But it is important to focus on the essentials that bless us and build up our faith. I often underline the things that I find difficult in the Word so that I will notice them and look at them again in due course.

2 Timothy 2:15 says:

> *Do your best to present yourself to God as one approved, a workman who does not need to be ashamed and who correctly handles the word of truth.*

We need to learn how to handle God's Word correctly and this will come with experience and diligence. This is why we need to go digging, to find the depth and breadth of it. Study will help us to do this.

4. MEMORIZE THE WORD

Many people find it difficult to memorize Scripture, but it is a very valuable tool to utilize. I know that people who did not grow up in a Christian home often feel they have a distinct disadvantage in this regard, because the Scriptures were never

read to them when they were a child and they didn't attend
Sunday School. Those of us who did grow up in a Christian
home tend to be more familiar with the stories in the Bible.
Be that as it may, I believe all of us can memorize Bible verses,
regardless of our background. Psalm 119:9–11 says:

> How can a young man keep his way pure?
> By living according to your word.
> I seek you with all my heart;
> do not let me stray from your commands.
> I have hidden your word in my heart
> that I might not sin against you.

I believe one of the real strengths of memorizing verses is that
you hide the Word deeper in your heart. Reading and hearing
helps us put the Word in our mind, but memorizing it hides
it deeper down in our heart; it becomes embedded in us.

Having Scripture on the inside of us is important because
when we are under pressure, we can easily draw on it and
put it to use. When you squeeze a sponge, the thing it has
been soaked in will come out. Similarly, when we are under
pressure and being squeezed, what we have put into ourselves
will come out!

We are all familiar with the story in Matthew's Gospel
where Jesus is put under tremendous pressure by the devil in
the wilderness. His immediate response is:

> It is written: "Man does not live on bread alone, but on
> every word that comes from the mouth of God."
>
> Matthew 4:4

Jesus was able to use memorized Scripture to stand against
the enemy's accusations. If we make an effort to memorize the
Word, then we can do the same.

Dawson Trotman[1] said, "I know of no form of intake of the Word which pays greater dividends for time invested than memorised Scripture."

Deuteronomy 11:18–21 says:

> *Fix these words of mine in your hearts and minds; tie them as symbols on your hands and bind them on your foreheads. Teach them to your children, talking about them when you sit at home and when you walk along the road, when you lie down and when you get up. Write them on the door-frames of your houses and on your gates, so that your days and the days of your children may be many in the land that the Lord swore to give your forefathers, as many as the days that the heavens are above the earth.*

The easiest way I have found to memorize Scripture is this: when you read the Bible and something clicks with you, memorize that scripture. Don't pick any old verse at random and tell yourself, "I must learn this!" At times when we are reading, a certain verse will jump out at us and we know that this is God's word to us at this moment. When that happens and you think, "Yes, that's good", write it down on a postcard and place it somewhere prominent. It might be your car dashboard, the back of your loo door or on your fridge, but every time you see it you will be committing it to memory.

I guarantee that if you keep doing that, by the end of a week or so, you will have learnt it, especially since the Holy Spirit triggered faith in you using that word in the first place. It will usually be a word that you need in that season of your life to guard against the lies of the enemy.

Interestingly, research shows that after twenty-four hours the average person is able to accurately remember 5 per cent of what they have heard, 15 per cent of what they have read, 35 per cent of what they have studied, 57 per cent of what they have seen, but 100 per cent of what they have memorized!

5. MEDITATE ON THE WORD

I remember my son asking me when he was young, "Why do we have to levitate?" and I replied, "No, it's *meditate*!"

Psalm 1:1–3 says:

Blessed is the man who does not walk in the counsel
of the wicked
or stand in the way of sinners
or sit in the seat of mockers.
But his delight is in the law of the Lord,
and on his law he meditates day and night.
He is like a tree planted by streams of water,
which yields its fruit in season
and whose leaf does not wither.
Whatever he does prospers.

If our five fingers represent these five different styles of interacting with God's Word, then to me, meditation is represented by the thumb. When you grip your Bible in your hand, your four fingers hold it on one side, and on the other side, supporting them, is your thumb. Meditation, the ability to chew over the Word of God in your spirit, is what supports all of our Bible interaction. The whole thing rests on it. We should meditate on what we hear, on what we read, on what we study and on what we memorize.

When you hear something from the Word that strikes you, take it away and meditate on it. Chew the cud. I am one of those people who like to chew things over. I pull them apart and put them together again until I'm satisfied that I understand. That's meditating. We need to let the Word go to work in us as we chew it over; we need to let it challenge us, move us, perplex us, bless us, even annoy and irritate us. The Word can do all of that. Meditating on the Word helps us fix it into our spirit. We memorize things to fix them in our brains, but we meditate to fix them in our hearts.

In several places the Bible encourages us to meditate on the Word day and night. I don't know about you, but naturally speaking I can't meditate day and night, twenty-four-seven. My spirit, however, must be able to because the Bible insists it is possible. My husband, Gordon, can confirm that I often wake up in the morning, having "meditated" on something all night whilst I was asleep, and I then sit down and write a sermon straight away while the revelation is fresh in my mind. It sometimes annoys him and he complains, "How *do* you *do* that?!"

The gift of meditation is such a wonderful thing and yet it has been so hijacked and stolen by the enemy. Many Christians are scared of the thought of meditation and don't even like using the word because they think it sounds suspicious and New Agey. But meditation is biblical and many scriptures encourage us to do it, dwelling on God's Word so that it lives in our spirit.

When meditating on a particular verse of Scripture, it is helpful to ask ourselves the following questions:

1. What is the meaning of this verse in its context?
2. What is its full interpretation?
3. How should this be applied in my life?

Psalm 1:3 says that the person who meditates on the Word is like a tree planted by streams of water which yields its fruit in season, whose leaves do not wither, and whatever that person does prospers. That is God's amazing promise for us as we meditate. Joshua 1:8 confirms this:

> *Do not let this Book of the Law depart from your mouth; meditate on it day and night, so that you may be careful to do everything written in it. Then you will be prosperous and successful.*

Meditation is a powerful mixture of prayer and reflection which God will really use to direct us and speak to us.

Here is one final quote, this time from Jerome:[2] "Ignorance of the Bible means ignorance of Christ." No one could have put it more profoundly. That's why I urge you to read the Book. Read it cover to cover and love it.

Notes

1. Trotman founded the Navigators in 1934, and through this worldwide Christian organization he supported various Christian ideals, including maintaining the basic disciplines of the Christ-centred Spirit-filled life and abiding in the Word of God.
2. Jerome (c. 347–420 AD) is best known as the translator of the Bible from Greek and Hebrew into Latin. He was also a Christian apologist.

CHAPTER 3

The Bible – My Giant Toolbox for Life

All of us have our personal preferences – our favourite colour, preferred walk, or special meal. These differences are not necessarily right or wrong but just what works best for us. This goes for reading the Bible too. We each have our favourite books and themes. While there is no prescriptive way to read and glean revelation from your Bible, there are skills and disciplines you can learn that can help you achieve your goal more effectively. By now you will have realized that I take a more practical approach to learning. We have already looked at how we can use certain disciplines like memorization, study or meditating on the Word to deepen our understanding of the Bible. But if we want to really plumb the depths of this amazing book, we have to be prepared to venture outside of our natural comfort zones. We have to be willing to approach the Bible with a fuller understanding and realize the vast dimensions of the effect this Word can have on our lives and society. This Word is not just a light to give us guidance or a source of comfort to calm our fears. We need to use the Word in all its applications and not just get stuck with our personal preference of how to read this challenging book.

Let us consider the Bible like this for a moment: a giant toolbox for life with a wide variety of tools that range from the general kit for the average DIY man to the specialist equipment needed by a craftsman for a specific purpose. Many people read the Bible with the narrow perspective of their personal need and so miss the broader depth and breadth of the power of the Word to transform a nation! Some people only read the Bible when they need guidance. They use their Bible like a roadmap and open it when they are feeling lost. This is like a tradesman only learning to use one small screwdriver from his vast toolbox. We need to realize that our Bible is a well-equipped toolbox, full of specialist tools for each season of life. Like skilled tradesmen, we need to learn to use the Word so that we are correctly positioned to thrive in every season. The Bible has the answer for everything in life if we read it correctly! Throughout this chapter I want us to learn how to recognize and use these specialist instruments hidden in God's Word. So let's start to explore some of these tools!

THE WORD OF GOD IS A SHIELD

Whenever we feel vulnerable, exposed or insecure, the Word of God can be a shield that protects us. Literally, his Word in our lives becomes our defence tool that creates a barrier of protection against all opposition and provides a safe place of refuge for us. Psalm 18:30–32 says:

> As for God, his way is perfect;
> the word of the Lord is flawless.
> He is a shield
> for all who take refuge in him.
> For who is God besides the Lord?
> And who is the Rock except our God?

It is God who arms me with strength
and makes my way perfect.

In Psalm 119:114 the writer says:

You are my refuge and my shield;
I have put my hope in your word.

And the author of Proverbs 30:5 says:

Every word of God is flawless; he is a shield to those
who take refuge in him.

What an amazing quality! Every time we feel intimidated, the Word of God is a shield for us to hide behind. It can protect us because it is flawless and there is no access point for the enemy. Elsewhere the Word of God is described as an anchor that we can trust because it is immovable and secure even when circumstances around us are uncertain.

So when you read your Bible, make a note of all those verses that are "shield" tools, words you can take refuge in, and make an effort to memorize some of them. Then, when circumstances overwhelm you, you can quickly take up your shield and defend yourself if you have done your homework! In these days, when banks and national economies are in meltdown, stocks and shares are crashing and pensions are failing, remember that the Word of God is still unchanging. His Word is our shield in times of trouble.

THE WORD OF GOD IS WATER

Immediately we have a totally different image for the Word of God from that of a shield. Water cleanses, refreshes and hydrates us. Water is the essence of life and creation depends on it. Water flows forth, runs in deep rivers and fills our oceans – it is limitless and has no solid structure. Only water truly satisfies our physical thirst; in the same way, only God can truly satisfy our spiritual thirst. As we look at creation, and study the power of water, we find that God has illustrated his relationship with us through the Word in such pictorial detail. There are so many parallels that can be gleaned if we take time to explore the mysteries of his Word. In Ephesians 5:25–27 Paul speaks about the Word being like water:

> *Husbands, love your wives, just as Christ loved the church and gave himself up for her to make her holy, cleansing her by the washing with water through the word, and to present her to himself as a radiant church, without stain or wrinkle or any other blemish, but holy and blameless.*

The Word washes off the effects of sin. It is like a shower, rinsing away the effects of our worldly culture. As we live life, we absorb attitudes without even realizing it and we get contaminated. Ungodly mindsets can take root and we adopt ungodly values. We get sullied and need daily washing in the Word to keep us spiritually sane and enable us to walk a life aligned with God's principles.

This Word renews our mind. I believe we all need regular brain-washing! Many of us have seen something impure, grotesque or violent, either inadvertently or intentionally, which has been locked into our memory. After that kind of experience we need to wash our minds. We do not want those images to remain in our conscious or subconscious thought life, so we need the pure water of the Word. When we take the Word by faith, it purifies us, but it also has the power to realign us for blessing. Wherever the Word goes out, it brings life and rejuvenates. The right word at the right time encourages the tired and weary, for this Word has impact. For God has said, "my word that goes out from my mouth… will not return to me empty" (Isaiah 55:11).

THE WORD OF GOD IS A SWORD

God's Word is so versatile! We move from water, a substance that has no specific form, to a sword – an object with a sharply defined structure and a definite purpose. Ephesians 6:17 says:

> Take the helmet of salvation and the sword of the Spirit, which is the word of God.

And Hebrews 4:12–13, a well-known passage of Scripture, tells us:

> The word of God is living and active. Sharper than any double-edged sword, it penetrates even to dividing soul and spirit, joints and marrow; it judges the thoughts and attitudes of the heart. Nothing in all creation is hidden from God's sight. Everything is uncovered and laid bare before the eyes of him to whom we must give account.

This sword has two areas of contact: it is a weapon to be used against the enemy, but also an instrument of precision to be used to circumcise our hearts. The former is to be used for combat; while the latter, like a picture of circumcision in the Old Testament, is more like a surgeon's scalpel which cuts away selfishness from our lives. God uses his Word to lay bare our most intimate motivations and attitudes in his presence.

Again, we discover that memorized Scripture is one of the ways in which we can use the Word as a sword, especially in times of confusion and battle. When confronted by Satan in the wilderness, Jesus countered his attacks with Scripture, saying, "It is written… it is written…"! When we feel confused or intimidated, we need to rehearse our promises and go on the offensive and wield Scripture like a sword. "If God is for me, who can be against me?… My God shall supply all my needs according to his grace in Christ Jesus… God has not given me a spirit of fear but a spirit of power, of love and of a sound mind… Perfect love casts out all fear…" and so on. Rehearsing Scripture (memorized or not) in this way uses his Word offensively like a sword.

We also need to pray, "Search my heart, O Lord, and see if there be any sinful way in me." In these times we allow the Word to discern and cut away selfishness and unholiness in our lives. The Word has the ability to dissect and challenge our innermost thoughts, to cut through the façade and expose the reality of the hidden life. We need to let God's scalpel cut away the infected areas of sin and woundedness from our lives so that we can be healed.

This Word can cut us to the core, but it is also a powerful weapon to overcome all the attacks of the enemy. Like Jesus in the wilderness, as we become skilled warriors able to handle this sword, the Word, we will win our battles of intimidation and torment. We will cut them off and say, "No, it is written… the *truth* is…!" We will be a mature army of mighty warriors able to use the sword!

THE WORD OF GOD IS A PLUMB LINE

His Word is a plumb line, a benchmark, a consistent standard.

Listening to the media and the voice of the church, one could get the impression that God seems to change his standards according to modern culture. But God and his Word are constant and totally consistent. His Word stands eternal, never moves and never changes. Isaiah 40:8 says:

> The grass withers and the flowers fall, but the word of our God stands forever.

This word "stands" here carries the sense of a plumb line. It doesn't simply mean it will be around for a long time, but it has the sense of setting a benchmark, a reference point which will remain true forever. God's Word is the truth and is eternally relevant. It is the standard, the plumb line against which all things are measured. Isaiah 28:17 says:

> I will make justice the measuring line and righteousness the plumb line...

God has sent out his Word and his decrees stand like the builder's plumb line. Unfortunately, many do not use that right reference point for their life choices. As we look at society we can see this crooked nature, especially in the area of sexuality. What is society's definition of purity? Well, people look at how everyone else lives, and then look at their relationships and say, "Compared to them, I'm good." Their definition of purity is reached by comparisons with others. But we can only truly judge our choices against absolute and real values. We need to go to the plumb line of the Word and measure our life against it and then see whether we are pure or not.

A lot of people don't want to acknowledge that God's Word is a plumb line because it makes them uncomfortable. Take Romans chapter 1, for instance, which addresses the issue of homosexuality. There are Christian homosexual groups who campaign for gay people to be accepted in the church without the expectation of repentance, healing or change because, they argue, God created all things. I disagree. We should accept gay people but we must not accept their behaviour. I believe the Bible sets out a plumb line, a benchmark, and I don't think I can side-step those scriptures. I don't believe that God has suddenly changed his mind. However, I don't support those who are militant and aggressive against gay people, because God loves all people. But the Bible is clear that God hates the sin that grips people's lives. He has set a benchmark and we don't have the right to move the plumb line just because society has.

So, seeing the Word of God as a plumb line does not present a nice, peaceful image like that of the water, but nevertheless it is important that in these politically correct days we understand the Word of God as our constant standard. In Deuteronomy 30:11–16 we read:

> *What I am commanding you today is not too difficult for you or beyond your reach. It is not up in heaven, so that you have to ask, "Who will ascend into heaven to get it and proclaim it to us so we may obey it?" Nor is it beyond the sea, so that you have to ask, "Who will cross the sea to get it and proclaim it to us so we may obey it?" No, the word is very near you; it is in your mouth and in your heart so you may obey it. See, I set before you today life and prosperity, death and destruction. For I command you today to love the Lord your God, to walk in his ways, and to keep his commands, decrees and laws; then you will live and increase, and the Lord your God will bless you in the land you are entering to possess.*

Forever and ever the Word of God will stand. This is our foundation stone, the truth against which we must set all our decisions. It is our standard for purity and integrity. It is our reference point that shows us if we are aligned correctly. His Word will highlight where we are compromising and making poor choices. Unless we use this plumb line we have no true understanding of what is "straight" according to God.

THE WORD OF GOD IS LIKE YEAST

Like yeast, when the Word of God enters your life, it just spreads; it fills everything and brings change. One Bible commentator described its influence as being similar to spraying a bottle of perfume which then diffuses to fill a whole room with its fragrance. In the Bible we read this kind of expression again and again:

> So the word of God spread. The number of disciples in Jerusalem increased rapidly, and a large number of priests became obedient to the faith.
>
> Acts 6:7

> But the word of God continued to increase and spread.
>
> Acts 12:24

The Word of God grows and spreads. It is out there moving, filling every space both in your life and in your community. Jesus commented:

> What shall I compare the kingdom of God to? It is like yeast that a woman took and mixed into a large amount

of flour until it worked all through the dough.

Luke 13:20–21

The effect of the Word of God in your life can be compared to the effect of yeast in a mixture of dough. The yeast will permeate the dough mixture and change the whole consistency and appearance of the leaven. Does the Word of God penetrate your lifestyle? How much does it fill your everyday decisions? Words have great power. Gossip can spread and bring "negative yeast" to people, causing division and disharmony wherever the words go. Or we can choose to carry powerful, life-giving words that release God's "yeast" into our communities. Just like yeast in dough, once these words enter a person's heart, they have the power to bring change and alter the person's attitude and reactions. So release his Word into lives around you and watch it spread and grow!

THE WORD OF GOD IS MEDICINE

Have you discovered the power of the Word as medicine for your body and soul? In Psalms and Proverbs there are many references to the Bible's healing and restorative power. Proverbs 3:8 says:

This will bring health to your body and nourishment to your bones.

Choosing a lifestyle aligned to his principles is like taking a powerful vitamin supplement – it has healing power. There have been times in my life when I have actively "taken" the Word of God, just like swallowing medicine. When recovering from a serious traffic accident, my bones were literally crushed and taking months to heal, but I took the promises of God and three times a day declared them over the broken bones. I let his Word do its healing work in my legs, and today I walk perfectly, but it took miracles and medicine to restore my legs! Or maybe your mind is tormented by fear and depression, and you need to command the peace of God to rule again. We need to apply the Bible to our lives and take it like tablets of salvation. We must eat the Word and live! Isaiah 50:4 says:

> The Sovereign Lord has given me an instructed tongue, to know the word that sustains the weary. He wakens me morning by morning, wakens my ear to listen like one being taught.

This Word also has the ability to comfort and soothe. In one instance it is like a sword, cutting us to the quick, but the next minute it is like healing balm. But the effect of the Word of God is not limited to only restore our own lives; it also has power to work *through* us. We can administer a word that sustains the weary. When we preach or teach, which aspects of the Word do we portray? We need to display the full tool-box with all the aspects of his Word. Some pulpits use the Word solely as the plumb line, challenging people's wrong choices, and so they sound harsh and critical. Other speakers prefer to discuss only the healing and kindness in the Bible, giving the impression that God is tolerant and unconcerned by our sin. But we must demonstrate both mercy and judgment when we preach his Word!

My ministry is called *Heartcry for Change*, and usually when I minister in a new church, I find I use the Word of God as a healing balm. First you need to use the Bible as medicine, to give the people hope, as there are so many broken people in our congregations. Once they have been restored and renewed by the Word of healing, you can then teach them about the warrior's sword because now they are strong enough to hold it. Then you can begin to apply the Word as a plumb line in their lives, because they feel loved and secure enough to align themselves with God's standards and not feel overwhelmed with failure.

God's Word can restore our souls, heal our bodies and comfort all those who are broken-hearted. Some of us need to prescribe ourselves a course of his healing medicine and allow his Word to touch our brokenness. His Word needs to work deep in the hidden places of our hearts and minds and restore us.

THE WORD OF GOD IS AN ARROW

Throughout Scripture we find that the Bible describes the Word as being "sent forth" or propelled like an arrow. It illustrates God's Word as going out like lightning. Have you ever received a specific word for yourself, and the moment it was released, it was like an arrow hitting its mark? I remember several years ago when Cindy Jacobs suddenly stopped speaking and asked me to come forward, as she had a word from God for me. At the time I was struggling with my ability to write a book, and although several publishers were pursuing me, I felt that I was incapable of the task. Suddenly in the middle of this service she said to me: "Rachel, write that book! Stop hesitating – it is God who is opening these doors, so go home and begin to write!" No one knew my struggle except God, but his word struck me as a lightning bolt that day, and I went home and began writing!

At other times I have picked up my Bible and been

amazed at the accurate precision of the Word. Recently we were in Australia waiting for the birth of my first grandchild. The whole family had gathered but the baby had delayed and my son, David, was due to return to the UK the next day. So I picked up my Bible and prayed and immediately read this scripture: *"While they were there, the time came for the baby to be born, and she gave birth to her firstborn"* (Luke 2:6). The Word was like an arrow – it hit my fear directly and I came to peace, and, yes, our granddaughter Leila Douglass was born when we were *all* there!

The Word illustrated as an arrow is quite a different image from the Word used as a sword. A sword is a weapon used in close, hand-to-hand combat, whereas the arrow is used in long-range warfare. It can strike at the heart with power from a distance! Psalm 107:20 says:

> *He sent forth his word and healed them and rescued them...*

Isaiah 55:10–11 says:

> *As the rain and the snow come down from heaven, and do not return to it without watering the earth and making it bud and flourish, so that it yields seed... so is my word that goes out from my mouth: It will not return to me empty...*

We must remember that the Word of God is an arrow, not a boomerang! In other words, once it is sent out, it does not bounce back empty: it always hits its mark.

THE WORD OF GOD IS A LIGHT

This is an aspect of the Bible that we are very familiar with, as we love to use the Bible for guidance. When we need direction we quickly turn to the Word, expecting God to shine his torch on our situation and show us what to do. We are even prone to "lucky dipping" in our Bibles, hoping to get the right promise quickly. God is often gracious and when we open our Bibles in this random desperation, we do receive an appropriate promise and are reassured. However, there is no guarantee that, if you just open your Bible and point to a scripture, it will be accurate for you at that time. We have all heard stories about someone desperate for a word who randomly opens their Bible, points and then reads a verse like, "the birds of the air will pick your bones"! I trust that we then have the sense to close our Bibles and realize that this was not a true word for our situation and we need to start again!

Psalm 119:105 is a famous passage which speaks about the Word being a light:

Your word is a lamp to my feet and a light for my path.

Here we see that the Bible provides two types of light: it is a lamp giving specific light for the immediate next steps for our feet, and it is a broad light revealing the general direction of our path. In other words, God through his Word can give us very specific, step-by-step guidance for our life, and also general instruction about the direction and choices our future should take. Depending on our season of life, God's Word has this ability to direct us very generally, keeping us on the path of his calling, or it can instruct us in great detail concerning each decision of our future.

Psalm 119:133 says:

Direct my footsteps according to your word; let no sin rule over me.

In these times of confusion concerning your future, expect the Word of light to give you direction. Once I was praying with a lady and I really wanted a specific word of guidance for her situation. Often God does give me these words, but on this occasion I felt nothing. Afterwards I asked God why and he said, "Sometimes I bring people to a crossroads and then I remain silent because I want them to stop and wait before they move on." I could immediately see this pattern in my own life. Often God allows us to come to those "crossroad" places and does not reveal the next step immediately. In these times he wants us to rest, communicate and trust him. It seems as though whenever we are faced with the challenge of many choices, we just panic and would rather try every option than wait, doing nothing. But if we stop, listen and trust God, eventually the light will shine and he will say, "This is the way, walk in it."

THE WORD OF GOD IS A FIRE

The illustration of God's Word as a fire has several applications. Psalm 147:18 says:

He sends his word and melts them; he stirs up his breezes and the waters flow.

Here the fire of his Word can melt our cold-heartedness and stir us with fresh passion. In Song of Songs 8:6 God's love towards us is described as a blazing fire:

> *Place me like a seal over your heart, like a seal on your arm; for love is as strong as death, its jealousy unyielding as the grave. It burns like blazing fire, like a mighty flame.*

In this well-known Jeremiah passage (20:9) the Word is described as the sense of fiery, prophetic urgency:

> *But if I say "I will not mention him or speak any more his name," His word is in my heart like a fire, a fire shut up in my bones. I am weary of holding it in; indeed, I cannot.*

And in Jeremiah 23:29 we read:

> *"Is not my word like a fire," declares the Lord, "like a hammer that breaks the rock into pieces?"*

God's hot Word confronts our complacency, challenges our disobedience and increases the fiery heat of his conviction, so that we respond correctly. So, this fire of the Word convicts us of sin and burns up all the dross in our lives. But this same Word burns with an intense love for us that can never be quenched. His Word is a raging fire of love for each of us that can never be extinguished – this love will set us ablaze! His Word stirs the latent desires of our destiny, motivating us to act! For Jeremiah, suddenly the Word burnt so strongly within him that he could not be silent any longer. The calling of God was a raging fire and he had to step out and do what he was made to do.

How amazing it is that our Bibles can be like water and fire at the same time! God's Word can be a fragrant perfume, but then a sword and a shield. What an incredible tool God has given us!

THE WORD OF GOD IS A HAMMER

In Jeremiah 23:29 the Word is described as a fire and then as a hammer in the same verse. His Word is an instrument of breakthrough. It smashes arrogance to pieces and overcomes all opposition. It challenges and confronts every attitude that stands against the knowledge of God. That is why the Bible is offensive to some, as it does not pander to our personal preferences!

In 2 Corinthians 10:4 Paul teaches that the weapons we fight with are not worldly, carnal weapons. Instead, God has given us divine weapons which have power for pulling down spiritual strongholds. The Word is a mighty hammer that can take captive every thought that resists the knowledge of God. But we have to pick up the hammer of truth and smash the lies of the enemy with it. We need to declare his Word, using it like a hammer: "There is going to be a breakthrough in our land. There will be a new hunger for the Word of God and his ways!" We must believe that ungodly laws can be overturned and that new standards of purity can be raised as we use his Word for breakthrough.

In our personal lives, where we see the hardened areas of unploughed ground in our hearts and minds, we need to allow the hammer to confront the rocks of unbelief and see a mighty breakthrough. So let us take the challenge of Hosea 10:12:

Sow for yourselves righteousness, reap the fruit of unfailing love, and break up your unploughed ground;

for it is time to seek the Lord, until he comes and showers righteousness on you.

When the hammer has done its work, the soil of our hearts is ready for the seed!

THE WORD OF GOD IS SEED

Again, this image of the Word being like a seed is very familiar. Jesus described it in this way in Luke 8:

> "A farmer went out to sow his seed. As he was scattering the seed, some fell along the path; it was trampled on, and the birds of the air ate it up. Some fell on rock, and when it came up, the plants withered because they had no moisture. Other seed fell among thorns, which grew up with it and choked the plants. Still other seed fell on good soil. It came up and yielded a crop, a hundred times more than was sown." When he said this, he called out, "He who has ears to hear, let him hear." His disciples asked him what this parable meant. "This is the meaning of the parable: The seed is the word of God."

Peter wrote in his first epistle (1:23):

> For you have been born again, not of a perishable seed but of imperishable, through the living and enduring word [Greek: sperma] of God.

A seed, although small initially, carries within it the incredible potential of growth and, ultimately, of abundant harvest.

This *sperma* Word is capable of impregnating our spirit, and making us pregnant with the purposes of God. We must receive his Word into our lives and make room for this seed of destiny to grow. As we spend time in the Word of God, these seeds take root in our hearts and then we will be able to watch them germinate, grow and eventually come to harvest. When God gives you a promise, it is always in seed form! He never gives you a tree with the fruit already showing. His promise is the seed of potential, but we have to plant, water and nurture it before we are able to pick the delicious fruit of the promise fulfilled! So cherish the seed of his Word and watch it grow!

THE WORD OF GOD IS BREAD

The Bible should feed and satisfy us like fresh bread. The following well-known Scripture emphasizes this:

> *Man does not live on bread alone, but on every word that comes from the mouth of God.*
>
> Matthew 4:4

In the same way that bread is the simple, everyday food in most cultures, so the Word of God should be the staple diet of our spiritual man. Given the choice between bread directly from the oven, or an older loaf from the kitchen, most of us choose the fresh, warm bread. In the same way, we need to examine our spiritual appetite for the Bible. We need to make sure that religious duty and ritual have not made this precious book stale bread in our mouths! Ask God to awaken your appetite for fresh revelation and eat from the banquet of his Word!

So these are just a few illustrations that describe God's

Word, and even as I am writing I can think of many more that I have left out! So when you read your Bible next, think about these different aspects and how you can apply them in your life. Do not limit the use of his Word to just being a tool for guidance. Now discover these new dimensions and begin to use the Word effectively. For when we understand how to grip this Word and use it, it will be a more effective tool in our lives. Let us be people who are responsible and skilled with the Word, who know how to use it and then speak it with clarity and authority.

Eat and enjoy!

CHAPTER 4

Can You See? Discovering Your Prophetic Gift

All over the world, whatever the economic status of the nation, there is a cry for supernatural revelation. Even our godless Western society is ready to consider a supernatural answer to the crisis of the day. Our police forces solicit the help of mediums to solve crime scenes and the health services have turned to alternative medicine for cures for chronic pain and mental health disorders. We are hungry for answers beyond our limited knowledge and so our bookstores are filled with "prophetic" books offering self-help, future forecasting, horoscopes and financial predictions for the year to come. Unfortunately our nations have turned their focus away from the Bible and look to occult sources and other religions for their answers to life.

In the midst of this season of a growing fascination with psychic revelation in our society, the church, rather than being a voice of direction, has lost its confidence and become silent or confused concerning spiritual issues. Many Christians are nervous about their ability to hear the voice of God for themselves, let alone for issues of national importance! This insecurity means we hesitate to speak the Word of God with boldness into the lives and situations around us. We have become blind and deaf, unable to see and hear the purposes of God for our lives and communities. But now is the time to rediscover our God-given gifts of revelation. God created us to be like him. We are made to "see" into the spiritual realms and know the heart of God.

WHAT DO YOU SEE?

The most pathetic person in the world is someone who has sight, but has no vision.

Helen Keller

At first this quote seems rather harsh, until you consider the person who said it. Helen Keller was blind and deaf most of her life, contracting a disease when she was nineteen months old that took her sight and hearing, but she never let her disability rob her of her vision for life. She was an author, a political activist, a lecturer and the first deaf and blind person to earn a Bachelor of Arts degree. She was awarded many accolades for her achievements, was named in numerous rolls of honour and has streets in several nations named after her. She lived life with great vision and never let her limitations become a restriction to her dreams.

In these days God is calling his people and asking us this simple question: *What do you see?* This was his cry to the prophets of old. Moses, what can you see? Jeremiah, what can you see? Amos, what can you see? After this question to each of these prophets, he then tests their ability to see beyond their natural outlook and get his perspective on the events in their nation. After one such conversation with Jeremiah, God commends his prophet and says in Jeremiah 1:12: *"You have seen correctly, for I am watching to see that my word is fulfilled."* So now God is asking his church today the same question: What do you see? Too often we are so overwhelmed by our circumstances that we have lost our ability to see anything! We feel harassed and overcome, but God keeps challenging us to look up and see what he sees. So what can you see? Can you see only danger and impossibility or can you see hope and a future? Will you allow God to touch your eyes and help you see what he sees? But how can we learn to see into these spiritual realms with accuracy?

A traditional Eastern proverb says:

> Your vision will become clear only when you look into your heart. Who looks outside, dreams. Who looks inside, awakens.

So the heart of this matter becomes the matter of the heart! What we perceive and how we see beyond our natural circumstances will be affected by our heart (or emotional and spiritual) condition. If our hearts get hardened through bitterness or other circumstances, this can affect our prophetic ability to see and hear. We must be ruthless with every issue that could damage our heart. Often unbalanced prophecy comes from people who have an agenda or have been hurt. In Matthew's Gospel we read:

> *"For this people's heart has become calloused; they hardly hear with their ears, and they have closed their eyes. Otherwise they might see with their eyes, hear with their ears, understand with their hearts and turn,*

and I would heal them." But blessed are your eyes
because they see, and your ears because they hear. For
I tell you the truth, many prophets and righteous men
longed to see what you see but did not see it, and to
hear what you hear but did not hear it.

Matthew 13:15–17

Here God shows us that if our heart is damaged and closed, we will have difficulty aligning our natural and spiritual vision. However, in order to appreciate these verses fully, we need to read this scripture understanding how our eyes and ears work together in the natural and spiritual dimensions. So let us read it like this:

"For this people's heart has become calloused; they
hardly hear with their spiritual ears, and they have
closed their spiritual eyes. Otherwise they might see
with their spiritual eyes, hear with their spiritual ears,
understand with their hearts and turn, and I would heal
them." But blessed are your eyes because they see both
naturally and spiritually, and your ears because they
hear both naturally and spiritually. For I tell you the
truth, many prophets and righteous men longed to see
in the natural what you see in the spiritual and natural
but did not see it, and to hear in the natural what you
hear in the spiritual and natural but did not hear it.

From these verses we realize we are a privileged people born to see in both dimensions. Some people only see in the natural dimension, as their hardened heart robs them of their ability to see accurately in the spiritual realm, and so they become spiritually blind. On the other hand, the prophets can only see in the spiritual dimension, unable to see the actual manifestation of their revelation as the physical time of breakthrough was still to come. But we are a blessed people able to see in both dimensions in our lives.

So if we are to live as these blessed people, able to see accurately in the spirit, we need to regularly check our vision for the following sight defects:

- **Double vision.** Are we confused, with no clear focus or conviction? Do we see with the eye of faith or are we tossed by the waves of doubt? Are we always uncertain about which way to go and what decision to make, as we cannot see a clear way forward?

- **No vision.** Are we unable to see beyond our circumstances and reality? Has our vision become totally dependent on our natural surroundings? Are we unable to see the God factor in our world? Are we blind to our spiritual heritage? Has all hope died so that we no longer want to believe that there is a spiritual landscape out there?

- **Restricted vision.** Are we looking at life through our biased viewpoint, limited by our prejudice or tradition? Have we become bitter and cynical so that everything we see has a motive or agenda and we have lost all trust and ability to see beyond the memories which haunt us?

If you find that you have these sight defects, you need to allow God to heal your heart so that you can awaken fresh vision from within your heart. Ask yourself, "What is the cry of my heart that needs to be awakened?" and then let God help you release this cry once again.

If you are going to be a person of revelation, then you will need to have accurate vision concerning the following areas in your life:

Yourself

You need to know who you are and what your distinctive cry is. If you lose your identity you will soon lose your mission and purpose. So ask God to give you a clear vision of *whose* you are and how much your God loves you. In the Judges chapter 6 we read that God spoke into Gideon's destiny as follows:

> When the angel of the Lord appeared to Gideon, he said
> "The Lord is with you, mighty warrior."
>
> Judges 6:12

But Gideon's view of himself was that he was the least of the least of the least. He saw himself as being at the bottom of the pile. But when God spoke to Gideon, he had a different way of looking at him. So will you let your past be past, look at your life with the eyes of God, and dare to believe that what God has started *he* will perfect and that he does things perfectly?

Your home and family

So often we can only see the negative heritage in our generations and family. We are too aware of the conflicts and pain but not the gifts and spiritual blessing in the family line. Ask God to give you a new vision of the legacy, spiritual characteristics and DNA in your family. If you are the first Christian in your family, allow God to give you a vision of the spiritual heritage that you are pioneering.

Your church and witness

Ask God to give you a clear vision of your position in the church. Remember, what seems so obvious to you is often your area of gifting and service. Often we can feel, "Why doesn't anyone do this?" The answer is, no one else can *see* it! What seems so obvious to you, is invisible to the next person! So often what you see is the gift you are to the body. So ask God to open your eyes in the church and serve.

Your community

Again, when you walk out into your community you will see areas of need. Note these areas, as so often they are the areas of your compassion and service where you can bless others. Take notice of the issues that you campaign about or feel strongly motivated towards. Discover the missions and activities to which you love to give money or which you dream about changing. These reactions are strong indicators of what you see with your heart and long to change with your life. These are the areas where you have spiritual vision, but do not get overwhelmed by the task! In Nehemiah 4:14 we read:

> After I looked things over, I stood up and said to the nobles, the officials and the rest of the people, "Don't be afraid of them. Remember the Lord, who is great and awesome, and fight for your brothers, your sons and your daughters, your wives and your homes."

Nehemiah looked at his city but kept a God-centred view of everything, even though his heart was broken by what he saw. He inspected every area of the city. He knew his city. He knew its pain and depths of need, and yet in the midst of it all he could cry, "God is great and awesome! He will fight for us and deliver us!"

OPEN THE EYES OF MY HEART

So we need to be a people with healed hearts ready to "see"and "hear" for those around us. We should draw down the sound of heaven to earth for the many who have lost the authentic sound of God in their life. So how do we begin this journey of revelation and become skilled "seers"?

All over the world the church is hearing and responding to the call of the Bridegroom of heaven, "Now is the time for intimacy." But this Bride is very insecure and she is not sure that she really knows the voice of her Bridegroom. So the Bridegroom of heaven is calling his Bride, the church, and drawing her to a place of communication with him where he will share with his Bride the secrets of heaven. In the Song of Songs 2:14 we read:

> *My dove in the clefts of the rock, in the hiding places on the mountainside, show me your face, let me hear your voice; for your voice is sweet, and your face is lovely.*

This is a direct call from God. He is calling us to come out of the hiding place of fear and into the place of intimacy so that we can learn to hear his voice. This is a place of vulnerability where we talk to God and let him hear our voice and see our face. This is the learning place of revelation. Increased communication with God will always increase our revelation knowledge of him. The more time we spend with God, the more we will be able to "download" the secrets of heaven. As we listen, we will grow in confidence and recognize the ways and the voice of God. John 10:4–5 says:

> *When he has brought out all his own, he goes on ahead of them, and his sheep follow him because they know*

his voice. But they will never follow a stranger; in fact, they will run away from him because they do not recognize a stranger's voice.

This scripture says that because we are in relationship with the Shepherd, we are guaranteed to recognize his voice! So you can be confident that as you give time to listen, you will hear him! As you increase your time in prayer, you will increase your revelation skills. Unless we communicate with God, we will never give him the opportunity to communicate with us. We must learn to give God time to speak to us! People of prayer always become people of revelation! Here is a wonderful testimony from Ireland, where a simple illustration with a rose and a word of revelation about "Summertime" changed someone's life:

Dear Rachel,

I'm writing following your visit to Athlone last Saturday with Helen. You are unlikely to remember (given that you meet thousands of women worldwide) that we met once before, at a Lydia Conference in Greystones, Co. Wicklow in 1998. On that occasion you bought 100 roses, a mix of white, yellow and red, and presented them one by one to us Irish women. I received a white rose along with the message of "a new name – Summertime". This was very significant for me at the time. Firstly, I never liked my name (June). My parents had married in June 1958 and I was born the following March – child of their honeymoon so they called me June. However, there was a negative side to all of that for my mother – who had not wanted a pregnancy and a baby in the first year of marriage (esp. as she was ill for the entire 9 months and I was a fussy baby!).

Anyway, I just wanted to share how much affirmation and confirmation I received from your ministry almost 10 years ago and how the Lord has continued to build on that during the past decade...

June M.,
Republic of Ireland, 4 February 2008

DEALING WITH HEART DISEASE

Most of us are not wilfully disobedient but just woefully hesitant. We do not obey the nudges and senses of guidance because we are terrified that it was our own "good idea" and not God's commanded instruction. So firstly, we need to get rid of all our inherent *unbelief*. Most of us do not really *believe* that God wants to speak to us, so we cannot hear him. We must change our thinking and instead start to believe that God does speak to *me*! In Hebrews 3:12–13 we read:

> See to it, brothers, that none of you has a sinful, unbelieving heart that turns away from the living God. But encourage one another daily, as long as it is called Today, so that none of you may be hardened by sin's deceitfulness.

We must get rid of all our insecurity and uproot this unbelief; otherwise, this heart disease will rob us of really knowing our God. This passage of Scripture shows us that an unbelieving heart will turn us away from the living God. You will never have good communication with unbelief in your heart, as you will always be facing in the wrong direction. God wants to *see* your face, but unbelief turns your face *away* from God. So make a decision to get rightly aligned in the presence of God to receive revelation.

We also read in Matthew 6:22–23 that it matters where we focus our eyes:

> The eye is the lamp of the body. If your eyes are good, your whole body will be full of light. But if your eyes are bad, your whole body will be full of darkness.

We need to be careful and ask ourselves the question, "Where am I fixing my eyes?" In these days of visually intensive media, sexual perversion and pornography, many of us have been exposed to images we do not want to see. Others get trapped by this bait and become addicted to these images and then realize that by watching these pictures you open gateways of darkness into your life. If we desire to have a body full of light, then we need to examine our eyes and make sure they are good! To be a prophetic people, we must have an eye of faith, clear from all guilt and shame. We need to be people who are discerning about what we watch.

As we discipline what we watch in the natural we must also learn to be those with a balanced viewpoint who can see both the natural and the spiritual in balance. In 2 Corinthians 4:16–18 we read:

> Therefore we do not lose heart. Though outwardly we are wasting away, yet inwardly we are being renewed day by day. For our light and momentary troubles are achieving for us an eternal glory that far outweighs them all. So we fix our eyes not on what is seen, but on what is unseen. For what is seen is temporary, but what is unseen is eternal.

For some of us, our poor ability to see has been caused not by pornography but by fear and doubt. We are so locked into our anxiety about today that we cannot see the bigger picture of God at work in the future. We are unable to hold the temporary and the eternal in balance. We are able to focus only on the trouble of today and not on the promise of breakthrough tomorrow. But if we are to be messengers of the prophetic word, we must learn to see past the trouble to the promise! This takes courage and trust, but it is essential if we are to become a mouthpiece for God. We need to learn to see into the invisible realm of the promises of God and know that with him it is possible.

DEVELOPING SPIRITUAL EARS AND EYES

Prophetic revelation usually enters our lives through two senses – our spiritual ears and eyes – and as a result, prophetic people are often called "seers". Although the ears and eyes are usually the main receptors of the prophetic revelation, any of the body's senses can be used to bring a prophetic message. People can smell aromas of flowers and gardens, speaking of the fragrance of God. Others experience the "hand of the Lord" and feel the weight of his hand on their shoulder. Still others have experienced the taste of honey or other flavours in their mouth as they have worshipped. God is able to communicate to us through colours, images, creation and life, but we need to have ears and eyes that are tuned to respond to his voice.

HOW DO I "HEAR" THE VOICE OF GOD?

Usually we do not hear an audible voice but just get an impression which comes as a random thought or maybe a faint nudge or reminder. As you acknowledge this sense, and trust that this thought is God speaking to you, and respond, and then find you were in the right place at the right time, your faith increases. The more you respond to these "sounds" of God and get it right, the more your faith just keeps growing each time you use it.

Years ago I was standing in my home doing my ironing when I felt God warn me that a new believer in our church was going to attempt to commit suicide. Just then this woman, Julia (not her real name), called and asked me to collect her daughter from the school bus and bring her home with me. The phone conversation seemed normal and Julia promised she would come by later and collect her daughter. However, my feeling of disquiet increased after this phone call until I was convinced I had heard God. I truly believed that Julia was planning to commit suicide. I tried to phone my husband but the office lines were busy, so I kept praying until the urgency was so strong that I phoned the local doctor's surgery. I tried to explain that I believed someone I knew was about to attempt suicide and could I have help, but they were not impressed that I had no proof except a word from God! In desperation I phoned the ambulance service and asked them to go to the home of my friend, and then finally I managed to contact my husband, who was able to drive to Julia's home and meet them there. (I could not leave the house as I had no car and a baby sleeping upstairs!) When Gordon arrived, he found the door locked and Julia on the floor, semi-conscious with alcohol and drugs surrounding her. The ambulance arrived and they were immediately able to pump her stomach and give her assistance. If I had not called the ambulance when I did, Julia would have died before they arrived, as there was a considerable delay before their arrival, due to heavy traffic. Today Julia is alive and well and serving God. The enemy wanted her life, but God gave revelation to save her. What a great God! We need to listen to his voice, as sometimes lives depend on it.

However, not all situations are quite so life threatening! I remember doing the washing up downstairs when I suddenly realized the house seemed very quiet. I then felt this nudge of the Holy Spirit saying, "Go upstairs now!" I quickly ran up the stairs to discover my two children, toilet-brush in hand with the toothpaste and other lotions, about to redecorate my bedroom! I arrived just in the nick of time to save my new wallpaper and myself from hours of cleaning! I was glad I listened to his voice that day!

HOW DO I "SEE" THE VOICE OF GOD?

Once in a lifetime you may see an open vision or a picture may appear on a wall and you "see" his voice. But usually we "see" the voice of God in our everyday life as impressions and images triggered by thoughts or words that are then accompanied by a series of graphic details or memories that conjure a scene. For example, as you read the word *aircraft* it immediately stimulates an image of a plane in your mind. But then if you read the words *rescue helicopter* the image of the type of aircraft you imagine needs to alter to now represent the new type of aircraft described by these words. In the same way, God speaks specific words to us and as we learn to connect each word, we are able to form a series of images which reveal the heart of God.

For example, I was in a meeting in Utica, New York, when the Holy Spirit spoke this word into my mind: *zebras*. I had no idea what zebras had to do with this women's conference at which I was speaking. Then I felt God highlight a woman to me and say, "I want to give her two zebras!" All day I avoided speaking to this blonde white woman about zebras, as the word had no context for me. Then at the end of the evening service I asked those who were unable to conceive children to come forward for prayer. This lady was the first girl forward. Suddenly I knew the "two zebras" were twins! As I said these words – "God wants to give you two zebras" – this precious woman crumpled and sobbed.

At that point her husband, a large African American, who had joined her for the evening service, came forward and said, "You have no idea what you have just said! We have been unable to have children and because of our mix, black and white, we have always had a private joke between us, saying, 'Let's make love and make zebras.' But the children have never come. We were getting desperate and asked God for a word – and this is our language! God heard our cry!" A while later I received this email entitled "2 Zebras arrive in New York":

Dear Rachel,

My name is Rebecca King, my husband Phil and I are members of Mt Zion Ministries in Utica, NY. I wanted to write you to tell you that we have received a miracle and to thank you for your obedience to the Lord. You were in town with us on the weekend of Mother's Day, May 2005. During the Saturday night service I was working in the bookstore when someone came to tell me that I needed to go to the altar for prayer because you had called out to those in the congregation who could not conceive. I was at the very bottom of my pit that evening; you see, my husband and I had tried to conceive for 7 years and in January of that year I had miscarried our first child. I often listened to your teaching on the *Hannah Hour* during the past few years and I understood her torment in a very real way. I had finally decided to surrender the thing I wanted the most. My husband and I discontinued fertility treatments in 2002. Then it happened; that night after 7 years of crying out to God for children, years filled with promises from the prophets in the house, visiting ministry, healing conferences... came down to you asking the whole congregation to pray for us and to commit to pray for the promise of God to be fulfilled in our lives. According to the Dr I conceived on Mother's Day, the day after you prayed for us. I laugh now when people say, "Wow, what a miracle! Rachel prayed and it happened!" – but they don't realize the years of agony and heartache it took to get to that "suddenly". On January 25th 2006 I gave birth to my little "Zebras", identical twins Francesca Judith and Bernadette Gean King. They were a full-term pregnancy, both weighing more than 6 lbs. Even my doctor had to comment on how "remarkable" it really was, since he himself knew the chances of me conceiving in the first place were slim. Rachel, please feel free to use this testimony of God's faithfulness to encourage the other Hannahs in the body of Christ who are waiting and hoping that God's timing is indeed perfect and that it is His purposes that prevail.

May God bless you and keep you,

Rebecca King, Philip King and our Girls!

These spiritual impressions are trained by spending time with God. Your ability to understand this language is developed during times of praise and worship, times of reading the Word and praying. All these activities create a conducive atmosphere where God can share his heart with you. God can speak in many ways and through different mediums. We need to learn to recognize his ways of speaking to us. For it is only as we learn his voice in the private place that we will become more fluent and confident in the public place.

One day as I was travelling to London to lead a national prayer meeting, I had this sense that I needed to sound a "Wake Up!" call. However, many people felt comfortable with the condition of the church and were concerned about causing conflict if we challenged people to arise and take responsibility. Knowing much of this controversy, I asked God to give me a sign if I was to speak and challenge these British comfort zones. At that moment the train passed a huge advertising board with the caption, *"Let the nation awaken to new power!"* It was advertising a new electricity company, but I "saw" the sound of God that day, and so I spoke!

JESUS IS THE SPIRIT OF PROPHECY

In Revelation 19:10–11 we read:

> At this I fell at his feet to worship him. But he said to me, "Do not do it! I am a fellow servant with you and with your brothers who hold to the testimony of Jesus. Worship God! For the testimony of Jesus is the spirit of prophecy." I saw heaven standing open and there before me was a white horse, whose rider is called Faithful and True.

In our desire to grow in our prophetic gift we need to remember that the testimony of Jesus is the spirit of prophecy. We are not trying to develop a technique but a relationship. We can only grow in the prophetic gift if we take time to be a lover of Jesus, our Bridegroom. We need to know who he is and talk with him. As we spend time with him, heaven will open for us and we will become a prophetic people!

Unfortunately we have been living in an era where we have lost our simple love for Jesus and so the prophetic gift has been lost in much of the church. But now a new prophetic season is awakening as God wants to open the eyes of his Bride to her supernatural heritage. In Revelation 2:7 we read:

> *He who has an ear, let him hear what the Spirit says to the churches. To him who overcomes, I will give the right to eat from the tree of life, which is in the paradise of God.*

This is the time for a new supernatural connection with heaven. God wants a church which has trained ears and eyes that can be his voice to the nations.

RAISING A "SAMUEL" GENERATION IN THE LAND

God wants to raise a "Samuel" generation in the land again. He wants a people who cry, "Here I am! Speak to me, for I am listening!" He wants a church with an ear to hear the Spirit's cry for the world's nations and people. As we read 1 Samuel 3:1–4, we can easily identify with the spiritual state of the nation of Israel:

> *The boy Samuel ministered before the Lord under Eli. In those days the word of the Lord was rare; there were not many visions. One night Eli, whose eyes were becoming so weak that he could barely see, was lying down in his usual place. The lamp of God had not yet gone out, and Samuel was lying down in the temple of the Lord, where the ark of God was. Then the Lord called Samuel. Samuel answered, "Here I am."*

Samuel was ministering to the Lord, so he was in the place of communication with God; he was a lover of God's presence. But there was no prophetic expectancy: the Word of God and revelation were rare in the nation and the older generation of prophets had lost their ability to see and train the next generation. But fortunately God's light of revelation was still burning in his house. Here we find Samuel resting in the presence of God, where he was ready and available when God called his name. So Samuel was able to immediately respond and say, "Here I am!" As Samuel connected with God and learned to listen, he began to hear him clearly. Immediately God trusted him with a word of prophetic significance for the nation! In verses 19–21 we read:

> *The Lord was with Samuel as he grew up, and he let none of his words fall to the ground. And all Israel from Dan to Beersheba recognized that Samuel was attested as a prophet of the Lord. The Lord continued to appear at Shiloh, and there he revealed himself to Samuel through his word.*

A new level of prophetic ministry had returned to the nation. Here Samuel had learnt to let his words and God's words come into perfect alignment. If none of Samuel's words fell to the ground, then they must have been 100 per cent God's Word, as only the Word of God has this power and accuracy. At the beginning of 1 Samuel 3 we read that the Word of God was rare in the land, but by verse 1 of the next chapter we read that a transformation had taken place. Now the Word of God was being heard in *all* Israel. Samuel had become a mouthpiece for God in his nation; there was no longer a famine of the Word of God in the land.

Like Samuel, we need to cultivate a new level of intimacy with God so that we open up the heavens again and accurately hear the voice of God for our nation. Samuel became a mature prophet. God spoke to Samuel and there was accuracy and consistency in his message. God's Word and Samuel's word became the same thing! Through Samuel the prophetic barrenness in the nation was turned and God's revealed plans and purposes were spoken into the nation once again.

RESTORING THE PROPHETIC VOICE IN OUR NATION

God is looking for us to be his mouthpiece again. It is time that our communities heard God's voice on the issues facing us. There is so much false prophecy in the nation, with a huge increase in tarot cards, psychic fairs and horoscopes. But the nation needs to hear the real God speak. In Amos 3:7–8 we read:

> *Surely the Sovereign Lord does nothing without revealing his plan to his servants the prophets. The lion has roared – who will not fear? The Sovereign Lord has spoken – who can but prophesy?*

As Christians we should not be surprised by world events and disasters but rather prepared and ready with a Godly answer! We are made to be the head and not the tail. It is time for us to discover our eyes and ears and be revealers of the plan of God to others. The true prophetic gift needs to be restored to the church so that we can serve the nation. All around us there is an increase in witchcraft and alternative prophetic activity; people are hungry for supernatural communication. But this is the hour for the church to rediscover its eyes and ears! God has promised us that we live in a time when our eyes will be blessed and we will see and hear the purposes of God. God created us to be able to see in both dimensions. We have this ability to see with both our spiritual and natural eyes. So now we need to learn to relate what we see in the spirit with what we see in the natural and then communicate it to others.

WHAT DO YOU SEE TODAY?

As we look around us it is easy to identify the pain on the faces of children filled with fear, the tension between a couple experiencing marriage difficulties or the suffering of a person struggling with cancer. But God asks us, as he did the prophets of old, *What can you see?* In Ezekiel 37:2–4 we read the well-known passage about the valley of dry bones:

> *He led me back and forth among them, and I saw a great many bones on the floor of the valley, bones that were very dry. He asked me, "Son of man, can these bones live?" I said, "O Sovereign Lord, you alone know." Then he said to me, "Prophesy to these bones and say to them, 'Dry bones, hear the word of the Lord!'"*

All around us we can see situations that appear like this valley of dry bones, but God asks us to prophesy to dead situations and bring life. God is asking his church, "What do you see for the broken? What do you see for the hurting? What do you see for the sick and dying? Do you have a word?" To prophesy into a situation basically means to proclaim God's spoken Word into the dead place, commanding it to do and be what God says it should be. God's Word is always *creative* and it brings life wherever it goes. So we need to release these creative words over our children, marriages, family situations, churches and neighbourhoods. We see this in the life of Abraham, who held onto his faith despite all the evidence that said he was mad! Here in Romans 4:17–21 we read about the struggle of Abraham's faith:

> As it is written: "I have made you a father of many nations." He is our father in the sight of God, in whom he believed – the God who gives life to the dead and calls things that are not as though they were. Against all hope, Abraham in hope believed and so became the father of many nations, just as it had been said to him, "So shall your offspring be." Without weakening in his faith, he faced the fact that his body was as good as dead – since he was about a hundred years old – and that Sarah's womb was also dead. Yet he did not waver through unbelief regarding the promise of God, but was strengthened in his faith and gave glory to God, being fully persuaded that God had power to do what he had promised.

Abraham understood that he needed to examine the facts but then "see" *"the God who gives life to the dead and calls things that are not as though they were."* Abraham was able to see beyond the visible and speak the creative word. Today ask God for this fresh grace to see beyond the facts and then to release the creative word of God into dead situations and see the valley of dead bones live. This is the destiny of the church, to be a people who see and hear and are able to call forth the promises of God. So rediscover your spiritual vision and then get ready to speak the Word of God into many situations and bring change. Let us stand up and be a people who see what God sees and speak into impossible situations to release life!

CHAPTER 5

Ready and Prepared to Speak His Word (I Hope!)

Too often, when the church speaks, no one is interested! The voice of the church has been perceived as dry, boring and irrelevant. But now, as a new prophetic church prepares to communicate God's Word with relevance and depth, we need to learn new communication skills. We need to be people of the Word and the Spirit, able to balance biblical principles with perceptive revelation. When people prepare to preach, they often fall between two stools of training and practice. The first group assert with false confidence, "The Holy Spirit will show me what to say at the time, so I don't need to prepare or read my Bible beforehand." But the second group tend to be over-diligent: "I must be well prepared, I must read every commentary and get my notes and PowerPoint perfect!" While the first group risk speaking nonsense, this second group can get so absorbed writing their notes in the library that they forget to spend time talking with God!

LOGOS OR RHEMA?

If we are going to deliver God's Word with power and effectiveness, then we need to learn to connect our love for the written Word of God with our passion for his revealed Word. In the New Testament there are two primary Greek words translated as "word". They are *logos* and *rhema*. The Greek word *Logos* occurs 325 times in the New Testament, an example being Hebrews 4:12:

> For the word of God [logos] is living and active. Sharper than any double-edged sword, it penetrates even to dividing soul and spirit, joints and marrow; it judges the thoughts and attitudes of the heart.

Generally the *logos* word is accepted as referring beyond a mere word to an expression, principle or concept. The *logos* word defines the doctrine and foundational principles of God. The Greek word *rhema*, on the other hand, occurs 73 times in the New Testament and is used in the following well-known passages:

> ... and the sword of the Spirit, which is the word [rhema] of God.
>
> Ephesians 6:17

> Jesus answered, "It is written: 'Man does not live on bread alone, but on every word [rhema] that comes from the mouth of God.'"
>
> Matthew 4:4

The *rhema* word, however, is understood to be the specific, inspired or breathed Word of God for a particular situation.

It is the uttered or expressed Word of God to a situation or person but will never contradict the *logos* word. So as we prepare to open our mouths, we must understand that the Word of God is more than reciting a few biblical truths – it is carrying a living message. So let us explore this "Word" further.

WHAT IS THIS "WORD" WE HAVE IN OUR MOUTHS?

The *Word of God* can be defined as an utterance or saying that may refer to a single act, the entire law, the gospel message, or even Christ personally. In the Old Testament *Dabar* is the primary Hebrew expression translated as the "Word of God". It has various meanings, but there are three particular aspects that are encapsulated in this word, *Dabar*, that demand our special attention.

The prophetic Word

The prophets claimed to deliver the "word of God" (Jeremiah 1:9). For this purpose they were commissioned (Isaiah 6:8). This word of God addressed human beings and demanded a response.

The legal Word

In the covenant law, God spoke the words of the law to Moses (Exodus 20:1; 24:3–8). The heart of the law is called the ten words (Exodus 34:28; Deuteronomy 4:13). The entire law represents the will of God and so can be called a single "Word" (Deuteronomy 4:2 KJV). This Word also demands response: faithful obedience will bring God's blessing while disobedience will lead to a curse (Deuteronomy 30:15–20).

The creative Word

God created the world by his Word (Genesis 1; Isaiah 48:13; Psalm 33:9). This world reveals God's majesty (Psalm 19:1) and thus extends the sphere of his revelation beyond his work with covenant Israel to all people. The Word is spoken of as if it were a person who directs the events of nature (Psalms 147:15–18; 148:8), saves (Psalm 107:20) and gives life (Ezekiel 37:1–4).

THIS WORD IS IN YOUR MOUTH

Having understood some of the depth and breadth of the Word of God, we now discover that God intends us to be his mouthpiece. He wants his church to speak this Word! In decades past, church leaders considered this Word too important to be given to the uneducated congregation and felt it was their duty to keep the Bible and the preaching of the Word of God away from the ordinary people. But God had already made the decision to trust us to be carriers of his Word. What a privilege! In Romans 10:8–11 we read:

> *The word is near you; it is in your mouth and in your heart... if you confess with your mouth, "Jesus is Lord," and believe in your heart that God raised him from the dead, you will be saved.*

When we worked with Reinhard Bonnke in Africa, I remember him boldly stating that "God's Word in my mouth has the same power as God's Word in his mouth." At first I was quite shocked by this audacious statement. As though sensing my silent questioning, Reinhard continued: "You are asking yourself, 'How can this be possible? Why is this statement true?'" Then he answered my question and declared, "The power is in *the Word*, not in the mouth!"

It is time to speak his Word, to know that we can be carriers of his Word of power and begin to change our communities and nation.

EAT THE WORD

But if *his* Word is going to get out, we need to ensure that *his* Word has penetrated our lives first. We need to cultivate a deep hunger for the Bible. In Deuteronomy 8:2–3 we read how God stirred a hunger for his Word in the people of Israel:

> Remember how the Lord your God led you all the way in the desert these forty years, to humble you and to test you in order to know what was in your heart, whether or not you would keep his commands. He humbled you, causing you to hunger and then feeding you with manna, which neither you nor your fathers had known, to teach you that man does not live on bread alone but on every word that comes from the mouth of the Lord.

I believe that God is provoking a hunger for accurate revelation during this season of hardship. As people begin to lose their luxury and security, they begin to hunger for a word of hope and comfort. We need to realize that not all of us will be given conference platforms, but all of us have an audience! So get ready to speak with power, and enjoy this testimony:

> I just wanted to thank you for the book signing
> yesterday. I gave the book as a thank-you present
> to a colleague at work who had helped me out on
> a school trip yesterday. I don't know her very well,
> but her partner died of cancer a few months ago and
> her 21-year-old son has kidney failure and doctors
> have just discovered lumps on his lungs. She herself
> has been having kidney problems. It has been a
> catalogue of suffering and yet she keeps going. She
> is a Christian and a woman of great love but she has
> been struggling. All the way through your sermon I
> just kept getting her name in my head and I got you
> to sign the card for her, Carol.
>
> Today she came into the staff room – eyes
> brimming with tears, she had just read page one of
> the meditations. She said it was an answer to prayer,
> to read words that spoke to her heart and a way into
> understanding God's word on this issue. It was so
> moving. She was deeply touched by your words.
> Thank you! This has encouraged her faith and my
> faith! What a loving gracious Lord we follow.
>
> L.M.

SPEAK THE WORD

In Acts 1:8 we read:

> But you will receive power when the Holy Spirit comes
> on you; and you will be my witnesses in Jerusalem, and
> in all Judea and Samaria, and to the ends of the earth.

The word "witnesses" comes from the Greek word *martus*. This is the word from which we get our English word "martyr". So we must be prepared to pay a price and die to our reputation and agenda when we release this Word on the streets and into the lives of ordinary people. As we have seen, this does not give us the option of being "politically correct". We cannot speak what is comfortable. We need to understand this challenge in Numbers 22:38:

> "Well, I have come to you now," Balaam replied. "But can I say just anything? I must speak only what God puts in my mouth."

We need to have this sense of being an oracle of God. We dare not speak our opinions, as we are a mouthpiece for the living God. So we should not be surprised when this causes offence at times! In Malachi 2:5–8 we read about the characteristics of those who should speak this Word:

> "My covenant was with him, a covenant of life and peace, and I gave them to him; this called for reverence and he revered me and stood in awe of my name. True instruction was in his mouth and nothing false was found on his lips. He walked with me in peace and uprightness, and turned many from sin. For the lips of a priest ought to preserve knowledge, and from his mouth men should seek instruction – because he is the messenger of the Lord Almighty. But you have turned from the way and by your teaching have caused many to stumble; you have violated the covenant with Levi," says the Lord Almighty.

God wanted his people to speak the Word of the Lord with a

sense of responsibility and reverence. We are not free to "speak our own minds" but our words must be God's instructions. Since the church has watered down these instructions to be "culturally sensitive", we have caused so much confusion and have lost our voice. God wanted the church to be a place where men could seek instruction and find supernatural wisdom to answer their needs, but too often our teaching has become so muddled that we no longer give people life. The church has become part of the problem, not the answer!

CREATIVE WORDS OF LIFE

In Matthew 12:34–37 Jesus challenges the religious leaders of the day:

> You brood of vipers, how can you who are evil say anything good? For out of the overflow of the heart the mouth speaks. The good man brings good things out of the good stored up in him, and the evil man brings evil things out of the evil stored up in him. But I tell you that men will have to give account on the day of judgement for every careless word they have spoken. For by your words you will be acquitted, and by your words you will be condemned.

We need to realize that our spiritual communication is more connected to our heart condition and spirit than to our intellectual capacity. Our heart attitudes will have a greater effect on what we speak than the level of our knowledge or academic status. To be a good speaker you need a healthy heart more than you need an intelligent mind! We all know that teaching is not just about the words we speak but also the atmosphere we release as we speak. So if our heart is diseased our words will be contaminated. So we need to have regular heart inspections! In James 3:1–2 we read:

> Not many of you should presume to be teachers, my brothers, because you know that we who teach will be judged more strictly. We all stumble in many ways. If anyone is never at fault in what he says, he is a perfect man, able to keep his whole body in check.

If we want to bring words of life to people, then there is a standard required before we can speak his Word. We need to remember we are not giving a lecture but we are giving of ourselves and so sharing our lifestyle as well. Our choices need to be God-honouring if the Word through us is to have credibility and bring life. This does not mean we have to be perfect before we dare to speak, but that we must be teachable and ready to change wrong behaviour! I remember when I first began to speak, I still struggled with my temper, especially when I felt insecure. I was so concerned that I could hurt someone with my anger if confronted in a negative way after speaking that I took advice from a fellow preacher. He suggested that I should have some counselling, and so for one year I travelled to a Christian counsellor who helped me face the issues that had wounded my identity. I was still preaching during this season but I made time for God to deal with the issues of my heart so that I did not damage people when I was under pressure. I am still not perfect but I believe that it is our availability, not our ability, that finally qualifies us to be God's mouthpiece. So step forward and *speak*, remembering that we all improve with time if we stay teachable!

READY – STEADY – *SPEAK!*

Although much of our speaking and sharing will be on a one-to-one basis with friends or in the workplace, we cannot assume that our speaking will always be in the private place. Most of us will be given an opportunity to share our faith in a small-group setting or even in a larger forum at some stage in our lives, so it is worth getting prepared.

So imagine: *you have been asked to speak!* Once the invitation arrives, most of us panic! What are we going to say and will we make sense? Are there skills that you can learn if you have not been to Bible School or spoken in public before? I was terrified when I was first asked to speak at a Christian Union meeting to twenty-five students in Leicester, but now, many years later, it comes naturally. So I promise you it gets better with practice. Here are some of the lessons that I have learnt over the years that have helped me communicate and learn to enjoy public speaking. Whether you are speaking to a small Bible study, meeting someone in a small group to discuss your faith or preaching to a church congregation, I believe preparation helps. When planning what I will say, I usually think in terms of the following four areas of preparation:

1. Revelation.
2. Information and content.
3. Illustration.
4. Application.

REVELATION

If you are not given a specific scripture or theme, then first of all pray and ask God to show you what he would have you speak about. Often a scripture will come to mind, or a thought from which you can develop a theme. I remember when I was first asked to speak at a church in Peterborough, I had this phrase going through my mind: "Go buy the field." So I spoke from Jeremiah about buying land to build in times of difficulty. What I did not know was just that very week, the elders had met to pray and talk about whether they should purchase land and build a church centre. So when I spoke this word, I confirmed what they had been feeling during this time of private prayer but had not yet shared publicly until then. So as you pray, note these "random" thoughts or phrases and then ask God to give you a theme or context from which to speak.

If, however, you are given a subject or passage of Scripture to expound, take some time to ask God to give you his emphasis or slant on the subject you have been given. I speak at so many conferences and am often given a title for the conference, but I always try to think outside the box and listen for the heart of God concerning the church and the topic. Also, ask God to give you a purpose for the word that you will share. Have an aim and a response in mind as you prepare, and have a specific goal of what you want to see happen in the lives of the people as a result of this word you will share. Then pray for the words of revelation that will be the keys of breakthrough and receive faith that you will impart more than words. Take time to get Holy Spirit strategy on how the people should respond to the word you bring. Will you give an altar call or take time to pray for the sick, and how will you stimulate faith for this response as you speak? In Romans 1:11–12 we read:

> *I long to see you so that I may impart to you some spiritual gift to make you strong – that is, that you and I may be mutually encouraged by each other's faith.*

One of the greatest privileges of speaking the Word of God to someone is watching that Word change their lives. The right word in the right season gives people the words of life that they need and so brings transformation! After I have spoken somewhere, I love receiving the emails which tell me what happened in the people's lives while I was speaking. I have discovered that so often it is the random thoughts or the coincidences that touch someone's life deeply and give them fresh hope or turn them back to God. Here is one of the stories that I have received from Andy, who gave his life to Jesus. My husband and I spent many journeys with him to and from Heathrow when he was our taxi service, and we often talked to him about Jesus. But there was a day when he heard a word that changed him! So enjoy this story:

> I am now a regular at Haven House (Church) and could not feel more at home there, even though the 1st visit was rather strange because the night before at about 4 a.m. I awoke and felt compelled to start reading Genesis 3. Nothing strange there, I know, but then at the church Bob Bennett stands up and starts talking about Genesis 3 and mentions Alan Vincent and yourselves, which I never really thought too much about. But afterwards Bob came over to speak with me and when I told him my testimony of how I had ended up at Haven House and the past meetings with yourselves and Alan and the fact about Genesis 3, it all seemed a bit coincidental. He then went on to say it was Alan who led him to the Lord in 1967, the year of my birth, and that he probably had not mentioned your names in a service for years, and to top that he also used to work for BT, my employer now! Enough to make me feel that it

was no coincidence I was there... I feel compelled to
say "thank you" to both you and Rachel and to let you
know that I am being baptized on Sunday 13th April
and the Lord really has just changed my whole life
completely, not least with the 4 a.m. wake-up calls
to suddenly read his words...

Andy, 20 March 2008

Often we have a preferred method of preparing a talk. Some
like to work from the place of revelation and prayer and then
research their content; others prefer to work on the structure
and content and then incorporate God's revelation and
application. Personally I think it is important to develop both
skills. But whatever your preferred method, I believe that it is
important to take time to hear heaven's heart for the church
or person you are speaking to. So once you feel you have a
"sense" of what God wants to say concerning the topic, it is
time to find intelligent and helpful content.

INFORMATION AND CONTENT

Now that you have an overall direction for your topic and an
emphasis and purpose in speaking, you need to find all the
supporting scriptures, read any relevant commentaries and
find the related information to form the content of your talk.
Take some time to research relevant quotes, statistics, news
items and so on which will all support your thoughts. Prepare
some personal information about yourself and include a
relevant introduction for those who do not know you. Decide
on whether you should produce notes in a handout format
or use a PowerPoint presentation. Look at other ways of
communicating your information, such as DVD clips, music

or other visual and media aids, especially if the audience is younger. Look at study guides to ensure you understand the context of the passage; look up any relevant background history of the era; study the references, examining any of the Hebrew/Greek words that could help. This often needs careful research and, depending on the subject, can be very time consuming. Whenever you prepare any type of word, try to adapt your content and style of delivery to be relevant to the age group, culture and circumstances of the people with whom you will be talking.

Remember that much of this research on the subject will be for your background information rather than for you to actually use when you come to speak. When planning how much information to include in your final talk, take your overall time given and then deduct some time for your introduction and the final prayer or response, and then divide your allotted time between information and illustration.

If asked to speak at a church service or conference, you should not speak for more than 40 minutes in any one session, allowing 10 minutes for a response time or questions. I tend to plan my time carefully so that I know I will be able to include all my main points in my given time. As an illustration, I would tend to divide my 40-minute time slot as follows:

- 5 mins: introduction of yourself and your topic.

- 25 mins: your main talk.

- 5 mins: a summary of your main points.

- 5 mins: outline your response and challenge.

- 10 mins: prayer ministry or questions & response time.

When you come to speak, you need to keep a balance between the revelation from the Word and the supporting information. Remember this is God's life-giving Word, so it should not come across as just like a lecture or reading from a textbook.

ILLUSTRATION

A good illustration is worth a hundred words, so they say! Often what people remember most are the illustrations, so choose them wisely! Take time to choose the right illustration as, if effective, it will earth the revelation and information from your talk into the everyday lives of the people who are listening. Choose illustrations that reflect your style of communication, are relevant to your topic and complement your personality. Good speakers will often collect relevant illustrations and jokes, as these stories become vital links that connect people's hearts with the speaker. Many speakers use humour to build a bridge between the audience and themselves, first making the people laugh and then challenging them with truth! Also it's often good to use personal testimony as you speak, as this builds a sense of rapport between yourself and the congregation. Make sure that your illustrations are a mixture so that they are applicable to both sexes, all ages, married people or single people, and a wide range of educational, social and cultural backgrounds.

APPLICATION

Even though we want our talk to have theological depth and to be "spiritual", we must make sure that it also has a practical life application, otherwise we merely educate people with religious knowledge. Do not speak in such abstract theological terms that no one can understand. Especially when speaking to the wider church, remember some people may be visiting with their family, having never read the Bible, or they may be a brand-new Christian. I remember in our church someone had just finished giving the church announcements about the Thursday Intercession meeting. As the person sat down after her notice, a new Christian in the congregation asked, "Can I ask a question?" She continued, "I have been coming to this church for three months now, and every week you talk about this meeting at this secret 'intersection', and no one has told me where it is or if I can come!" She had never heard the word "intercession" and had no concept of what we were talking about! I realized then that, like most clubs and groups, we have our short-hand terms and specialist language and we need to explain the practical terms and definitions for words like "sanctification", "justification", "eschatology" and even words like "righteousness" and "holiness", as so many people have no context for these words today.

Whether you are prophesying in the church or preparing the talk for a men's Bible study, these principles apply: keep your language relevant and simple, and explain complicated terms. As you close your talk, summarize your main points and make sure you give people an accessible practical response that they can develop as part of their lives. Recently I spoke at a conference on the attribute of courage, and how God wants us to be courageous during times of hardship. I spoke about the challenge to Joshua, "Be strong and be courageous… do not be afraid!" and then asked people to examine the areas where they had lost hope and begun to feel fearful concerning their circumstances.

As I watched the faces of those listening, I realized God was speaking to people in a deep way, so I ended my talk more quickly than planned and asked people if they would like prayer. It is important to allow time for people to pray and respond to the Word. I then used the scripture where Jesus walks on the water towards his disciples and says to them, "Take courage. It is I. Do not be afraid!" As we prayed this over those requesting prayer, many were in tears as God deeply touched the pain and fear in their lives. I believe that the Word of God does its work and brings healing and life. So take time and let people have some space to personally apply the Word before they run out the door and are confronted by their busy lives once again. Sometimes you may feel a corporate declaration is appropriate, and you could write something for display and then ask the people to stand and say it with you. Or you could summarize the aims you had in mind when you prepared your message and let the people discuss their response and resulting action in small groups. This often works well when considering community action and our evangelistic response.

So you have opened your mouth and spoken; now relax and watch his Word do its work! In 1 Samuel 3:7 we read:

Now Samuel did not yet know the Lord: the word of the Lord had not yet been revealed to him.

But this is a new day when the Word of the Lord will be revealed… God wants us to speak! He has called us into the secret place so that, unlike Samuel, we can know the Lord and through us the Word can then be revealed. As you read the Bible and especially the prophetic books, you will notice these phrases appearing again and again: "the hand of the Lord came upon me … the word of the Lord came to me"! The prophet Ezekiel uses this second phrase fifty-seven times in his book. This was his lifestyle. So get ready! This is the day for the Word of the Lord to come to us and then through us! God is raising up a prophetic generation who will once again speak his Word!

CHAPTER 6

A Prophetic People with Good Manners!

So we are ready to open our mouths, carry his Word and speak. But how does the prophetic ministry work most effectively in the local church to release the hidden destiny and callings of the people? How do you use the prophetic gift wisely but fearlessly to challenge and provoke but at the same time encourage and strengthen? If we are going to use these gifts of revelation effectively in our local church, then we need to study them in more depth.

SHINE AND MANIFEST

This passage in 1 Corinthians is a textbook reference when wanting to study the gifts of the Spirit:

There are different kinds of gifts, but the same Spirit. There are different kinds of service, but the same Lord. There are different kinds of working, but the same God works all of them in all men. Now to each one the manifestation of the Spirit is given for the common good. To one there is given through the Spirit the message of wisdom, to another the message of knowledge by means of the same Spirit, to another faith by the same Spirit, to another gifts of healing by that one Spirit, to another miraculous powers, to another prophecy, to another distinguishing between spirits, to another speaking in different kinds of tongues, and to still another the interpretation of tongues. All these are the work of one and the same Spirit, and he gives them to each one, just as he determines.

1 Corinthians 12:4–11

The nine gifts mentioned in this passage are called the "manifestations" of the Spirit. Here this word "manifestation" literally means to show forth, to exhibit, and to shine with. So as we carry these gifts we should shine and demonstrate to our friends what the Holy Spirit looks like. We should realize that these supernatural gifts can also have a natural counterpart – the gifts of healing has medicine, prophecy has teaching and so on. We also need to appreciate that these natural gifts can become channels through which the supernatural power of God can be released. This passage also reminds us that there is a variety of expression, but the same source and the same God. Here the word used for "variety" means diversity. So we should expect different people to use the same gift of the Spirit in different ways.

As we study these nine gifts of the Spirit, it is easier if we divide them into the following three groups:

Revelation gifts

- The word of wisdom
- The word of knowledge

- The discerning of spirits

Speaking gifts

- Prophecy
- Different tongues
- Interpretation of tongues

Power gifts

- The gift of faith
- The working of miracles
- The gifts of healing

REVELATION GIFTS

These gifts all reveal something: either divine strategy for a crisis, or accurate knowledge of a past event, or detailed information about the spiritual atmosphere in a place. So let us dig further:

The word of wisdom (WOW) (verse 8)

This is a "what to do" gift or a "what will happen" gift. A perfect biblical illustration is found when Solomon discovers the true identity of the baby's mother by using supernatural wisdom. A word of wisdom (or, as I like to abbreviate it, WOW – as this gift amazes people and makes them go "Wow!") is a supernatural revelation given by the Spirit which releases divine strategy concerning the purposes of God for a situation. A word of wisdom frequently offers a solution to solve current issues or gives advice concerning a future event.

These words can come as spoken prophecy, dreams, an audible voice, visions, or just in a normal conversation. God also gave the early church supernatural strategy for the next phase of their church growth. The disciples had realized that it would not be right for them to neglect the ministry of the Word of God in order to serve the growing community of widows and poor in their midst, so God gave them the strategy for another layer of leadership, called deacons, to help them!

The word of knowledge (WOK) (verse 8)

This is a "what is happening" or "what has happened" gift, and Jesus demonstrates how to use this gift when he speaks with the Samaritan woman at the well in John chapter 4. Here, using the word of knowledge, Jesus is able to show this woman that he understands her, as he knows about her failed marriages. The word of knowledge (my abbreviation is WOK, as this gift stirs things up!) is a supernatural word of revelation concerning present or past activity. There are many examples of the word of knowledge in Scripture, but I love the story where the king is so irritated by the accuracy of Elisha's use of the word of knowledge that he really believes Elisha must have a spy in his bedroom (2 Kings 6)!

The discerning of spirits (DOS) (verse 10)

Many would define the discerning of spirits as the ability to name, describe and identify the operation of evil spirits alone. But I believe that we should also expect the discerning of spirits to give us revelation and insight into both the angelic and demonic spirit worlds. In 2 Kings we read that Elisha was able to discern God's protection and "see" the array of angels sent for his protection. People often use this term in a broader sense too when they speak about the discerning of attitudes and motives. It is the God-given ability to judge a matter and to distinguish between right and wrong or truth and deception.

SPEAKING GIFTS

The gift of prophecy (verse 10)

Prophecy is the declaration of God's thoughts, not in the exact words, but coloured by the prophet's character, personality and culture. We are told that we should desire this gift more than the gift of tongues, as it brings greater blessing to the corporate body as it is understood by all (see 1 Corinthians 14:1, 5). The Hebrew word translated as "prophecy" literally means to "flow forth", while the Greek word means "to speak for another; to speak as a representative of". So to prophesy is to flow forth with God's word as a representative of heaven.

The gift of tongues (verse 10)

He who speaks in tongues "speaks in divine secrets", according to Weymouth's translation of the New Testament. This gift is the supernatural ability to speak an unknown or unlearnt tongue. In 1 Corinthians it is described as a gift full of wonder (14:2) and is given to edify the believer and should primarily be used as a devotional gift. This gift is strongly linked to prayer and assists us in developing a two-way communication with God. Although your tongue may be unknown to you, you may find on occasion that someone else will recognize your tongue and be able to tell you which language you are speaking.

The interpretation of tongues (verse 10)

This is the supernatural revelation of the meaning of the tongues. It is not an exact translation of the tongues and the interpretation may be more concise or longer in length than the original tongue. Even if you did not bring the original message in tongues, you should feel free to bring the interpretation if you receive it.

As we begin to use these gifts of revelation, they start to change the way we speak, pray and worship. So we will study the role of the prophetic word in more detail in Chapter 7, the use of prophetic prayer and intercession in Chapter 8, and the emergence of prophetic worship and the Psalmist's ministry in Chapter 9.

A fuller study of the 1 Corinthians 12 gifts would normally also include a detailed explanation of the power gifts listed above. However, the focus of this book is on the communication gifts rather than the demonstration gifts, so although I really believe in the demonstration and power gifts, I have limited myself to discussing the communication gifts here.

CAN I PROPHESY, PLEASE?

These gifts of the Spirit are available for all. There is no elite club, and the Bible encourages us to *"Follow the way of love and eagerly desire spiritual gifts, especially the gift of prophecy"* (1 Corinthians 14:1). So get hungry and ask God to fill you! Generate and create an atmosphere of expectation in your life. Expect God to speak to you and expect him to speak through you, giving you accurate words for someone else. So start to learn the voice of God, identifying the range of the ways in which he communicates with you. Discover how to recognize the "God ideas" and stop dismissing them as just your own thoughts. Try to carve some time out from your schedule and use it to be still and train your ear to listen. Then break the sound barrier and speak, and you will be amazed at how God will use your life and his words to bless many! So read this testimony and enjoy!

I joined my friends at the Norfolk Showground in Norwich at a Christian Bible week, Monday 14th August, as a day visitor… The evening meeting was taken by Rachel Hickson who spoke about prayer briefly before encouraging us to turn into groups of 6 around us so that we could practise her teaching… We all prayed simply when suddenly I was captured by this statement from the stage and I simply heard these words: "Be healed; every muscle, every ligament."

We continued praying for many things that evening as directed by Rachel and I left for home feeling uplifted. In fact, the next evening we went back again… and then I started to notice that things were different. I was walking easier; my hip was not pulling or protesting at all. The Wednesday was spent shopping in Cambridge all day and I got back about 5-ish. On Friday I spent the day at school working and on Saturday I arose early in time to get to the car boot sale at 7 a.m… the rest of that weekend was spent at a 60th birthday party, Church and socialising. I spent Monday at work again and then we packed for our holiday. Two weeks after "that Monday", I told Nick about the amazing miracle and 3 weeks on, it's still OK. I have tested my hip big time.

I have dug the garden, fetched, carried, lugged and heaved tonnes of car boot stuff. I have sat and sat at my computer and rose without stiffness or panting or puffing after long periods... If you can remember, buttock and leg were under-developed and balance was a huge issue for me. No longer does it feel that my leg/hip is going to fail or let me down – it is incredible! I am so thankful to God! 6–7 weeks later and it feels perfect... I am mindful nearly every day of this miracle.

Joyce C., Mildenhall, Suffolk

SKILLS OF DELIVERY

Most of us are terrified that we will humiliate ourselves if we dare to prophesy and so following these guidelines could save you from embarrassment. So let us learn the following:

Timing

Giving the right word at the wrong time can ruin a meeting or mean the word is not received in the way it should be. Too often we can sense the prophetic urgency and rush to share the word and miss the moment. We need to remember that the Bible says, *"The spirits of prophets are subject to the control of prophets. For God is not a God of disorder but of peace"* (1 Corinthians 14:32–33). So do not be concerned if you need to wait some time before you can bring your word, but relax and wait for your opportunity.

Tone

Use you normal voice and language when you speak. Sometimes people feel that they should use a strange religious tone since they are speaking on behalf of God, but usually people find this off-putting and so do not listen. Do not shout and sound angry as again people get frightened; just use your normal volume and minister with an attitude of love and grace, even if the prophetic word is challenging and direct. Do not be heavy-handed but gentle when giving a prophetic word, especially if it is being given personally to an individual.

Style and method of delivery

Should the prophecy be sung or spoken? Sometimes the atmosphere of music will increase the impact of the word. Should you use an illustration to demonstrate the prophetic word? Make sure you use the correct gift of revelation for the task. Should you use a word of wisdom or knowledge combined with the prophetic word? Be careful about the length of your word. Do not repeat the same thought again and again but learn when to stop. This all takes practice!

Most of us have many memories of strange "prophetic" moments. I remember being in a church service when the person prophesying said, "God wants to come as a roaring lion..." He then promptly fell on all fours and began to roar at the top of his voice. All the children began to scream, people walked out and finally the ushers had to ask him to please be seated. Even if the word was valid, the style of delivery was so strange that people were terrified and unable to listen.

CHECKING THE CONTENT

Once you know how to speak, you then need to discern what God is asking you to say! So here are some guidelines to help you decide on what is appropriate prophetic content:

Prophecy strengthens, encourages, comforts

> *But everyone who prophesies speaks to men for their strengthening, encouragement and comfort.*
>
> 1 Corinthians 14:3

Sharing a prophetic word is not the place to air your personal grievances, disguised as speaking for God. I remember one instance when a man stood up and shouted across the church, "God says 'Shut up!'" Unfortunately this person was unhappy about some of the changes being proposed and he decided that he would "prophesy" his annoyance. We laugh, but we must make sure that our words bring strength, encouragement and comfort to those who listen.

Prophecy builds up the church

> *Since you are eager to have spiritual gifts, try to excel in gifts that build up the church.*
>
> 1 Corinthians 14:12

So the prophetic word should not tear down and destroy but should help to give structure to, reinforce and strengthen what God is building. Like a good spiritual vitamin tonic, the prophetic word should edify and help the church towards healthy growth.

Prophecy challenges and brings the correction of sin

> *But if an unbeliever or someone who does not understand comes in while everybody is prophesying, he will be convinced by all that he is a sinner and will be judged by all, and the secrets of his heart will be laid bare. So he will fall down and worship God, exclaiming, "God is really among you!"*
>
> 1 Corinthians 14:24–25

We need to remember that it is the goodness of God that leads people to repentance, so that even if a prophetic word exposes people's needs, it will never happen in a way that humiliates them. Often people will feel that all the inner sins and secrets of their hearts are being revealed even when you are not targeting anyone specifically. Just by being in a prophetic atmosphere people become aware of their sin!

Prophecy brings direction concerning future events

> *A prophet named Agabus came down from Judea. Coming over to us, he took Paul's belt, tied his own hands and feet with it and said, "The Holy Spirit says, 'In this way the Jews of Jerusalem will bind the owner of this belt and will hand him over to the Gentiles.'"*
>
> Acts 21:11

Here Agabus gives Paul an accurate word concerning his future and what would happen. This was not an easy word for Paul, and although the people around him tried to alter his decision, Paul received the word as direction instructing him to go to Jerusalem rather than as a warning, and so he went.

It is also interesting to note here that Agabus used a prophetic illustration to portray his message.

Usually you should only deliver correctional and directional prophetic words once you know you have the approval of your leadership and you are trusted to bring words that are accurate and helpful. But as you prophesy be as specific as possible, even with timing where appropriate, but always be prepared to admit if you get it wrong.

RIGHT RESPONSES: THEY HAVE PROPHESIED

So you have received a prophetic word – what should your response be?

Discern it

Before you make any decisions or take any radical actions to move house or change your job, you should take some time to pray and confirm that you believe it is a word from God. Does the word bring you peace, hope and joy? Does it confirm what you have already been sensing in your times with God? Prophetic words should receive a confirmation in your spirit. Let them direct you but do not base your life upon a word because of the prophet's reputation if it does not sit right within your spirit. We are told that we should weigh prophecy in the following passage: *"Two or three prophets should speak, and the others should weigh carefully what is said"* (1 Corinthians 14:29). I believe that the reason we need prophets to judge the prophetic words is not only to discern whether they are false or true words but also to help us to discern the implications and applications of the prophetic word given.

Respect it

When God speaks we must acknowledge it and then obey. We need to give his word priority in our lives and our services. If you are leading the meeting, do not just continue as if God had not spoken. Honour the prophetic word and ask God to show you how to lead the people towards an appropriate response. If the prophetic word is given to you in a personal context, try to write it down before you forget it. Try to keep a record or journal of the words spoken over the life of your church and use these to encourage the church to pray. Do not interpret prophetic words according to your own agenda. I was asked to call a pastor after a word I had given to a girl caused him concern. When I phoned him he asked, "Can I confirm that you prophesied over 'Sandra' that she can leave her husband and marry her boss?" I was shocked and said I would never prophesy such a thing. So we decided to visit this woman together and ask her why she thought I had prophesied this. When questioned, she responded immediately, "But you said, 'God will give you the desires of your heart', and I want to marry this man!" We need to treat God's word with respect and not extract parts of it out of context to serve our own desires.

GOOD PROPHETIC PROTOCOL

The answer to abuse is not non-use but correct use...

Arthur Wallis

All through this chapter I have tried to teach some basic house rules that apply when ministering in the prophetic gift, as I believe that good etiquette is essential if the prophetic and the pastoral team are going to work together with respect in the church. Unfortunately the prophetic ministry has often earned itself a bad reputation as being flaky and unruly. So we need to develop a protocol alongside training so that people can feel secure.

DECENTLY AND IN ORDER, PLEASE!

We are instructed to ensure that things are done *"decently and in order"*(1 Corinthians 14:40, NKJV). But as you train the prophetic you quickly recognize the tension between creating an atmosphere of freedom while maintaining a sense of order. Prophecy has these two dimensions of being both a spiritual inspiration but also a developed skill. So, as with any such discipline, there is a need for boundaries of practice and understanding to be in place, both for the security of the one prophesying, and for the protection of the recipient, as the training and development of the gift grows. In 1 Corinthians 14 we can read a summary of Paul's apostolic wisdom concerning the correct use of spiritual gifts in the public setting. We need these boundaries and they should not be viewed as control mechanisms but rather safety nets that will catch you and save you from harm!

Good prophetic protocol needs to be put in place and understood as a foundational part of the prophetic practice in the local church. When prophetic words are given to the church leadership they should not come with a harsh, corrective style but with a respectful and accountable tenor and language ("I think, feel, believe..." etc.). The leaders should make time to meet with the prophetic people in the church by creating a real environment of trust where good accountability can be established. This should not happen on a corrective basis only, but should be part of an ongoing regular relationship where training, trust and input are given. This will help an atmosphere of security and trust to grow between the leaders and the prophetic ministry and so enhance the gifting in the church.

DIRECTIVE AND CORRECTIVE PROPHETIC GUIDELINES

There are certain areas of revelation which I believe we should handle with great caution. Although I cannot say you should *never* prophesy into these areas, I would be very hesitant to speak into these areas without proper accountability and a witness present. Below is an outline of areas of directive and corrective revelation where I believe we should be careful and get pastoral advice before we speak:

Directive revelation

- Marital status (marriage/divorce/engagement/"going out").
- Pregnancy, sex of child, and words for children.
- Major financial decisions.
- Change of location (house/area move).
- Changes in employment.
- Direction in ministry.
- Issues of structure/direction for the church.

- Any matter with serious repercussions for a person if wrong.

Corrective revelation

- Any statement that seeks to reveal or renounce sin or unrighteousness.

- Any analytical word making assessment of attitude, motive or action.

- Any revelation that may cause division or endanger relationships.

If God does reveal information about any of the above-mentioned situations, I would proceed with caution but only after you have chatted it through with a leader. It is always better to be cautious than damage people's lives with good intentions!

GIVE AND LET GO

Another area which is always a danger zone for prophetic people is learning to release yourself from your word. Most of us experience the difficulty of "letting go" of a word which we have been passionate about if we do not see it endorsed. Often in our desire to see the word recognized we can be tempted to manipulate, coerce or campaign to get a response. But once the word is given, the responsibility of the word is with the hearer not the messenger, so you must let go! Also remember, there is always a degree of limitation in every prophecy as *"we know in part and we prophesy in part"* (1 Corinthians 13:9). We may think that "our" revelation is the answer to everything but remember, we only have a part of the whole!

CHARACTER MATTERS

Just because you have a prophetic gift does not mean you have to be weird to live with! Remember that one of the tests of authenticity is the actual life of the prophet. There is no mandate or excuse for unreasonable, eccentric, or over-emotional behaviour. We need to act and react in a Christ-like manner and so earn the right to be heard and trusted. Jesus demonstrates this with his life. He is 'the Word made flesh' and his character and life choices were in perfect alignment with his message and proclamation. We do have to walk the talk, not just speak it! This is the day for a new prophetic generation to rise up and be supernaturally normal, carrying the presence of God wherever we go!

CHAPTER 7

Prophetic
or Pathetic
Ministry?

What do we mean by this term "prophetic ministry"? Most of us have our personal views about the prophetic ministry ranging from indispensable to dangerous, based on our experience or stories we have heard. Many of us have heard terrible tales of prophetic disasters where a "prophetic" person has visited a church and given a word instructing someone to marry a particular man or sell their home and move to the mission field, with the result being a catalogue of disasters. But equally we have heard the testimonies of those who had amazing breakthroughs after a specific word: a baby that is born to an infertile couple, an inheritance that is released to a financially crippled family. So there are plenty of stories concerning the prophetic out there, some wonderful and others terrible! Does the prophetic ministry still have a part to play in the church in the twenty-first century? How should the prophetic function in the life of everyday church?

UNDERSTANDING THE PROPHETIC MINISTRY

Just because the prophetic ministry makes us feel uncomfortable, that does not necessarily mean that it is wrong. It may challenge our preferences of ministry style but this does not give us the right to dismiss it outright as erroneous. We need to learn to distinguish between the unauthorized fire of natural hysteria and the true passionate fire of God that reawakens the call. I believe that you can receive direction and specific words for your life when you are in the atmosphere of the prophetic ministry; you do not need to have someone personally call you by name and give you a prophetic word. Sometimes we do not even realize that we have been in a prophetic atmosphere but we do experience the benefits. Here is a testimony of a man who heard a word and then found it confirmed the passion he had in his heart:

> On a previous visit by Rachel Hickson to Lancaster I was given a word by Rachel about God's calling on my life. One of the things she felt was that I should look back into my family line and see what gifting was there – what were the natural skills and abilities and things that were just "in the blood". I felt a little confused afterwards and explained that my Grandfather had been a technical designer, something that my father is skilled in, but I was just in the process of leaving a 10-year career in graphic design but felt a call to music!
>
> Although I felt God was in it, I shelved the word for a good six months and did nothing about it, until my curiosity got the better of me and I decided to delve a bit further into my family line. I

paid some money to the National Archives to retrieve information from the 1901 census where I tracked down my Great Grandfather. He was in fact born just 20 miles south of here in Preston, but the census puts him in Sheffield in 1901 where his full-time job is listed as "musician". It turned out he was a band leader and his band even played for a royal visit of King George V!

I'm not going to lie – I had tears in my eyes when I found the page with this information! I have always loved music and play a number of instruments but always felt like it was just something I did and very much on the "B" list of my priorities. The word that Rachel had for me gave a validation to what my true passion is, and brought something in me to life. Since then there has been much more of an authority in my playing too and a sense that this is what I have been commissioned to do. My life has gone from something of a treadmill to a brilliant adventure. Our Father knows the true desires of our hearts!

Mark

For me, these are two of the indicators that you have been in a prophetic atmosphere:

1. Revelation

It releases an atmosphere of revelation in your life and suddenly brings clarity into your circumstances so that you can "see" beyond the seen! You will find yourself having conversations like this: "Oh – now I see and understand what has been happening to me! It all makes sense…" You do not need to have received a personal prophetic word but the atmosphere gives you context and explanation for what you have been experiencing in your life, even if the sermon did not specifically touch any of these issues. You find yourself saying, "Now I can *see!*"

2. Context

You find you have fresh understanding of your destiny and your season of life at this time. Suddenly you can find a context for and understanding of the trials and the journey that you have been on. You are able to get a sense of the big picture of your life. You will find yourself exclaiming "Oh, now it makes sense. I recognize this season. *This is that!*" The prophetic words and promises that you have had begin to fall into place and you realize that you are walking the journey of the prophetic fulfilment. You find yourself saying, "Now I can *understand!*"

All of us should carry the spirit of revelation and prophetic insight as part of our inheritance. We are all made for supernatural revelation and communication. Many times we can experience a real prophetic flow and revelation in a meeting, but if there is not adequate prophetic training in the church we can get hurt by people's enthusiastic inexperience or, worse, outright deception. People do get hurt and confused by prophetic wildfire that is unaccountable and so we do need to be teachable as we become these mouthpieces for God. But worse can be this, that in our excitement of receiving accurate prophetic words we can create an atmosphere where people go prophet-hunting rather than God-chasing. Good prophetic ministry should always make people hungrier for God and not create a celebrity atmosphere for prophets. You should walk away from a prophetic atmosphere more determined to become a seeker of God, knowing that seekers do become finders! The prophetic atmosphere should be like that smell of freshly baked bread and stir in you a great desire to visit the bakery, the throne room of heaven!

A PROPHET OR A PROPHETIC MINISTRY?

Just because you have a proven track record and are able to flow with good prophetic ministry, it does not necessarily mean that you are a prophet, however much you prophesy! I believe that we need to understand the difference between carrying a mature prophetic anointing and holding the office of a prophet. The prophet has a governmental position given to them as recognition of their prophetic gift and their leadership. This governmental position is given first by God and then publicly recognized and confirmed by the church. We cannot just elect ourselves to the office of "prophet", but we are given this honour by others. A prophet has the role and responsibility within the local church to train the people to use their spiritual ears and eyes, helping them discern the spiritual environment over their lives and the places in which they live.

When a prophet or mature prophetic ministry is functioning in the local church context, you should see a congregation grow that knows how to worship, enjoys the presence of God and communicates with heaven; people who understand the gifts of the Spirit and how to use the gifts of revelation; a church that is able to discern the spiritual climate of their area and pray with authority into situations. The prophetic gifts and spirituality of the prophet should be reproduced and developed in the lives of those who connect and are trained prophetically in the church by them. The fruit of all good ministries is that it should bring forth life and reproduce itself wherever it goes. So prophetic ministry should not produce little elitist groups with an arrogant air of "we hear God and you need to listen to us" but rather an open excitement that embraces the presence of God with an expectation that God will speak to us as we listen! I believe that we need more of these prophets in our churches today so that we can be a voice to our communities.

THE ARCHITECT AND BUILDER AT WORK

In Ephesians 2:19–22 we read:

> *Consequently, you are no longer foreigners and aliens, but fellow citizens with God's people and members of God's household, built on the foundation of the apostles and prophets, with Christ Jesus himself as the chief cornerstone. In him the whole building is joined together and rises to become a holy temple in the Lord. And in him you too are being built together to become a dwelling in which God lives by his Spirit.*

In verse 20 of this passage we see that the foundation depends on the apostolic and the prophetic gift working together in cooperation. I like to think of the prophet as the architect and the apostle as the builder working together in harmony to produce a secure house with firm foundations. The prophet functions like an architect in the house of God. He walks into an area and looks at the land and then looks at the resources and receives an impression of what could be built in that area. Whereas a natural architect uses his natural gifts and skills for inspiration, a prophet is inspired by the Holy Spirit and so is able to reveal God's plan for that person, church or neighbourhood. The prophet is able to produce a blueprint plan from heaven; he is able to describe the model of the "building" and give the church and leaders a clear vision of what the prospective project should look like. As he prays God reveals to him the plan and purpose for this community. It is like having the architect arrive at your door with the plan for your dream house; you can see it and at last have a clear vision of the potential and possibilities!

Although this is so exciting, we have to remember there is no house yet, there is only a plan! For this we need a builder – the apostolic gift! Too many times we get so excited about the potential of the prophetic promises of God, but unless someone comes alongside to help us build the dream, the promise will never become a reality. This is why in good church the apostolic must work with the prophetic. Often these gifts tend to compete rather than cooperate with each other, but when they do work together securely there is no greater joy! Once the prophet has revealed the plan, then the apostolic can position the people to build and make it happen. Initially the sharing of the vision will bring fresh hope and new expectancy, but if no one builds and works with the project, then disappointment and hopelessness grip the people. Another dream comes to nothing! So, as the apostolic comes and takes the promise and makes it happen, people will give themselves to the work. However, people will need the ongoing prophetic encouragement at this stage as once you start to build, it is hard work and people grow weary! So the prophet and the apostle need to work together, constantly bringing vision and encouragement with the practical outworking and reality unfolding.

THERE IS A PROPHET IN THIS HOUSE

Having a prophet in the house is a little like having a resident interior designer in the church! They are able to bring healthy changes and presence into every area of church life by discerning the atmospheres and attitudes and brightening church life with the "right" colours. A prophet should be able to bring vision and direction into all the areas of church expression by helping the departments focus correctly on the vision for maximum effect. The mature prophet should be able to reveal the architect's plans for your personal life but also for the church and even the nation. However, we must recognize that different prophetic people work at different levels of revelation and accuracy in these various areas, depending on the grace of their gift. Romans 12:6 says:

> We have different gifts, according to the grace given us.
> If a man's gift is prophesying, let him use it in proportion
> to his faith.

We need to ensure that the prophet is working within their realm of grace and gifting and we must not pressurize them to produce revelation. One of my most challenging times is when I have preached for an hour and have then been involved in prayer ministry for a further two to three hours, and I begin to feel exhausted. But the desperation of the people wanting a word or prayer motivates you to keep going longer, and then you meet someone who will not let you go. They say something like, "I *know* you have a word for me and I need you to pray and give me a word!" You have nothing left inside you except a feeling of exhaustion; you are struggling to hear God over the tiredness of your body but you now feel pressurized to produce a word so that you can leave. I have learnt that this is a real danger zone and it is better to run than to give a false word! We need to understand that there are different levels of grace, gifting and faith when operating in the prophetic gift. So we should help people discover these boundaries of their gift so that they are always functioning from their position of maximum strength.

WHO AM I?

In Matthew chapter 16, Jesus asks his disciples, "Who do you say that I am?" Here Jesus wants to discover what gifts and ministry the disciples see in him. Do they see a prophet or just an ordinary man? Have they discerned that he is the Son of God? When Peter makes his famous declaration – "You are the Christ" – Jesus commends him for seeing with the eyes of revelation and looking beyond the usual assumptions concerning his life. In Matthew chapter 13 we read that Jesus is in his home town of Nazareth and there confronts a resistant atmosphere towards him that withholds the miraculous. In verse 57 Jesus explains this principle, that a prophet is often without honour in his home town. Unfortunately, because Nazareth could only see Jesus as a local carpenter's boy, this familiarity had undermined their faith and so limited the flow of miracles in their town.

We, too, need to be able to recognize the prophetic gift of God anointing a person, especially when we know them well. Especially as parents we need to be ready to release our children into their calling and not limit them with our familiarity. To you he may still be "little Jonny" but now in the kingdom of God he is an anointed worship leader. To the church she may still be "Daphne who makes tea" but in the Spirit she is called to be on the mission field changing nations! We must not let familiarity rob the calling of God that rests upon the lives of those around us. So often in church something will be shared by the Pastor and others and then a visiting speaker will come and preach, maybe even from the same passage of Scripture, but definitely on the same theme, and everyone will be amazed and excited. Why could they not hear it before? They were too familiar with the vessel and so lost the message! So do not let familiarity rob you of the prophetic gifting in your life and church.

DECLARE THE WORD

The prophet is called to be a mouthpiece of God and so should deliver this message with authority. God's Word in your mouth has power to create and change situations. Often I have wondered how speaking a word can bring change. Then when reading Psalm 107:20, "He sent forth his word and healed them; he rescued them from the grave", I noticed that the sent Word of God has the power to heal. So what is in this Word? As I considered these things I felt God speak to me about the power of the sound of his Word to bring change.

We are all familiar with the principle of an opera singer hitting a high note with perfect pitch and shattering a wine glass with her sound. If this is possible in the natural, just imagine the power in the spiritual domain. The solid glass just shatters at the sound of her voice! In a similar way, impregnable circumstances must yield as the Word of God is released. But we need to train our ears to hear the sound of heaven and then release this Word with perfect pitch so that it hits its mark.

We are also familiar with the technique of ultrasound

where we target kidney stones with sound waves to disperse the stones and bring healing to the body. These ultrasound waves need to be at the right frequency to hit the specific stone and then disperse it. God has the perfect words, at the right frequency, so that we can release them to destroy cancer and growths. God is calling us to send forth his Word, like these ultrasonic beams, and watch his Word shatter disease.

> About 2 years ago you were speaking here in Ottawa. We were about to leave when you called all women who had problems conceiving etc. to come forward. You specifically mentioned those that needed prayer for healing of fibroids! I came forward because 3 months earlier I had lost a baby because of a fibroid. At that time I was deciding whether to have the fibroid removed or to try again for a baby. During the prayer we were in a circle and with my eyes closed I felt the person praying for me take my hand and place it on the left side of my lower belly which is exactly where the fibroid is. Fast forward...
>
> On January 8, 2004, I delivered a healthy baby boy and the fibroid didn't cause any problem throughout the pregnancy. Thank you for allowing God to use you. Just for *me* you again prayed for healing of fibroids! Thank you!
>
> K. D., 2 April 2005

We need to listen to God's voice and then *speak* the Word with authority and watch the Word do its work.

MAKING OTHERS LOOK GOOD

In Ephesians 4:11–13 we get a glimpse of what heavenly church looks like. Church is designed to be the place of lifting each other up so that each one fulfils their potential:

> *It was he who gave some to be apostles, some to be prophets, some to be evangelists, and some to be pastors and teachers, to prepare God's people for works of service, so that the body of Christ may be built up, until we all reach unity in the faith and in the knowledge of the Son of God and become mature, attaining to the whole measure of the fullness of Christ.*

Here the Greek word translated "built up" is *oikodome*, pronounced "oy-kod-om-ay", and it has this sense of having the understanding of the architecture, and an ability to construct and build the structure! In other words, one of the ways people are equipped to do God's work is by releasing the prophetic and apostolic gifts to work together in the local church to help people find their true identity and purpose in God.

The prophetic ministry brings an acceleration of understanding and enables you to move forward with fresh confidence concerning the times and seasons in your life. I believe that good prophetic ministry is vital in a church as it is sent to equip, train and release people. It has the unique gift of stirring, irritating and positioning people and resources in the right place for the right time. It should see ahead and help people plan their lives to be in the right position spiritually and naturally to fulfil their destiny. The prophet's job in local church is to teach and train people to recognize the "God sound" in their lives and identify their God-given spheres of influence and then help them to be released to do what they are made to do. The role of the prophet is to make other people look good! There is nothing more satisfying than living a life that you know is secure and centred in the purposes of God for you.

Although the prophetic will function in helping to build the lives of individual people, it can also help position the whole body of the church with purpose and vision. So for example, if God begins to speak a word into the body concerning *healing* and the leaders confirm this is God's direction for the church, the prophetic gift should function by bringing advancement into this area of church life by:

- Discerning spiritual areas of resistance and strongholds.

- Bringing words of revelation concerning healing and miracles.

- Activating increased prayer and prophetic authority to change the spiritual atmosphere.

However, the prophetic gift should also work with the other four ministry gifts outlined in Ephesians chapter 4, and help them understand the priority and grace upon their gifts in this season of healing. So the prophetic will pray and bring revelation to the…

- Teachers – by helping them write courses which teach and train the church how to pray for the sick.

- Apostles – who begin to build and prepare a strategy for an expression of healing in the church and on the streets.

- Evangelists – by praying for new authority to use healing as a tool of Good News.

- Pastors – by asking for words of revelation and wisdom so that the church is prepared pastorally, particularly to care for the sick. The pastors should be prepared with information and instruction to equip the church to understand and walk in their healing, but also be ready to help those who are not yet healed keep their hope.

Good prophetic ministry should bring more than just accurate revelation into your life; it should also help you position your life to activate and live this word too.

REVELATION, APPLICATION AND IMPLEMENTATION

Receiving an accurate prophetic word is always a "sweet and sour" experience for me. At first you are blown away by the goodness of God who gives you such amazing promises – this is the sweet part; and then you feel overwhelmed by the responsibility and practicalities – this is the sour part! Many times I have received a word and after the initial glow of gratitude, I have felt terrified. How can I do this?! For this you need prophetic help. In the local church setting the prophetic ministry should help you take the word of revelation and then work with you so that you can break it down into everyday application, direction and wisdom. Each prophetic word consists of three parts:

- Revelation.
- Application.
- Implementation and context.

It is often difficult for us to correctly assess the application and implementation of a word for ourselves, as we have our own natural biases of how we think the word should be fulfilled.

We can usually establish if the revelation is correct but it takes more maturity to discern the areas of application and context. One's ability to correctly determine the application and context surrounding a prophetic word shows the measure of maturity of the prophetic gift. Most of us get it wrong sometimes in our lives but God is still faithful!

For example, while in Birmingham, over seven years ago now, I gave a prophetic word to a lady that went something like this: "In six weeks from today God will open doors for you so that you can fulfil the dream you have carried for over fifteen years. You have longed to work with teenagers and God says to you today that the time of waiting has ended; so get ready! In six weeks it will be all change and new doors will open and God will fulfil your desire to work with children." This was the revelation part.

As I gave this word the woman began to sob and cry. Afterwards she told me that she had had a dream of working with teenage boys from broken homes and backgrounds for seventeen years. She had received this calling when she got saved but her husband was still not a believer and so she lived constantly hoping he would get saved so that she could fulfil this ministry. I asked her to keep in contact, as I had given her a very specific word with a six-week time-frame. However, I heard nothing and it was three years later that I met the same woman at another conference and she came and told me this story.

Indeed, six weeks to the day her life changed, but not as she expected. She thought the word meant her husband would get saved in six weeks, but instead she returned home to find a letter confessing a long-term affair and divorce papers. She was horrified but the divorce went through and she was left comforting her own boys as their father left home. However, she kept looking at this word and wondering whether God

PROPHETIC OR PATHETIC MINISTRY?

had known this and how she could minister to teenage boys from broken homes now. So she decided to help her own boys through this tough time and kept talking to them as they processed the loss of their Dad. The school, aware of the situation at home and noticing how well the boys were coping, asked this mother if she would be prepared to come and talk to other pupils about divorce and Dad leaving home. This happened, and before long this mother was asked to speak at other schools and assemblies.

Eventually the local council, noticing what this mother was doing in the schools, asked if she would be willing to help in some after-school activities for young teenage boys with emotional issues. Finally the council gave her a property where she could have a home for teenage boys with emotional problems! Last time I talked with this mother she said, "At first I hated that word but today I can see the revelation was 100 per cent accurate, but my application and implementation of the word was wrong. I thought I knew the context and how God would fulfil his word and I got it wrong, but today I can see God has been faithful!"

So when we receive a word of revelation for our local church, "that God wants to bring healing to the house and there will be signs and wonders", we should also pray and ask God to give us any detailed instructions about how this revelation should be structured within the church. Maybe God will give you details of what this breakout of healing will look like and how people can activate this word both personally and corporately.

CHARACTERISTICS OF A PROPHETIC PERSON

A prophetic person is a presence person! They love the presence of God, are easily connected in the place of prayer and worship and find it a place of refreshment. All the Old Testament prophets were also men of prayer and out of this place of intimacy their revelation flowed. We see this especially in the life of Daniel. As a result of this, prophetic people will often need times of reflection and being alone with God so that they can hear, be replenished and then receive words of revelation for their situations.

Prophetic people discern heart attitudes and are sensitive to atmospheres, and so can feel that they are just suspicious and negative if they are not heard or understood. They can quickly pick up conflict and disunity. Gordon often calls me his "sniffer dog", as prophets are revealers. They have a gift for uncovering hidden things and exposing sin. You often find people begin to tell you things and then exclaim, "I don't know why I told you that. I have never told anybody about this situation before!" Prophets also have the ability to explain riddles, interpret dreams, make unclear problems obvious and give you wise solutions.

Since prophets are presence people, they often live with a thin veil between heaven and earth and can experience both angelic encounters and demonic confrontations. For them the supernatural world is close and they speak both into the natural and supernatural realms. They often carry an unusual authority for specific miracles and a breakthrough anointing to release faith for people who are weary. One of the gifts of the prophet is to bring encouragement. Prophets carry the Word with fire and passion. They tend to speak with a sense of urgency. Like the prophet Jeremiah, you sense the cry that they are speaking because there is a word shut up in their bones!

ELIJAH OR MOSES: TWO MODELS OF PROPHETIC MINISTRY

In Scripture we have two types of prophetic ministry illustrated by Elijah and Moses the prophets. These two models have different spheres of influence and are different expressions of the prophetic ministry. Although Elijah and Moses both had specific functions in their nation, we find that the models of their ministries lived beyond their lifespan. On the Mount of Transfiguration (see Matthew chapter 17) Moses and Elijah both appeared and were talking with Jesus, and Jesus later explained to his astonished disciples that the Elijah ministry was still to come. Then again, in Revelation 11:4–6 we read:

> These are the two olive trees and the two lampstands that stand before the Lord of the earth. If anyone tries to harm them, fire comes from their mouths and devours their enemies. This is how anyone who wants to harm them must die. These men have power to shut up the sky so that it will not rain during the time they are prophesying; and they have power to turn the waters into blood and to strike the earth with every kind of plague as often as they want.

Here we can quickly identify these two olive trees as Elijah and Moses: Elijah is the one who has the power to shut up the skies and prevent rain, and Moses is the prophet known for "every kind of plague". So let us look in more detail at what these two models of the prophetic ministry represent:

Elijah

At the time of sacrifice, the prophet Elijah stepped forward and prayed: "O Lord, God of Abraham, Isaac and Israel, let it be known today that you are God in Israel and that I am your servant and have done all these things at your command."

1 Kings 18:36

The Elijah prophetic ministry tends to speak at a national level or concerning national events. This prophetic ministry tends to be itinerant, as they are sent to particular places with specific words, often amongst governmental people with detailed words for the nation. They can be seen as loners but they are known as a voice to the national scene. Although connected with a local church, they find their main sphere of ministry is outside their church, not within it.

Moses

Since then, no prophet has risen in Israel like Moses, whom the Lord knew face to face.

Deuteronomy 34:10

This is a prophetic gift mixed with a leadership role within the local church. This prophet works closely with people, helping and giving them strategic vision that enables them to step into their full inheritance. They are prophets who carry a sense of having been in the presence of God, where they hear his strategy and then come down from the mountain of intimacy and work with the people. They teach people the ways of God and his desires for them. They carry a prophetic authority and move in signs and wonders on behalf of the people. They can touch heaven and change earth!

As we examine these two types of prophetic ministry illustrated in Scripture, we then need to recognize their expression in our churches. Some people carry these definite distinctives, while other ministries may carry a mixture of these two types or may even have a season of one model followed by a time functioning as the other kind. But we need to realize that there are some prophetic people who are called to travel and function on behalf of the church in the world, more in the Elijah model, while others are called to be in the church and train the people to function with revelation in the world, more like the Moses model. In these days I believe that God will begin to advance the prophetic ministry in the church for those who have ears to hear, so that we can be an informed church ready to act intelligently in our communities.

HOPES, DREAMS AND ENCOURAGEMENT

When the prophet is finished, you should be able to see with more clarity, be able to build more strategically and carry a fresh sense of peace and joy! The prophetic gift should leave you encouraged and ready to face your world with excitement. We read in Acts 15:32 that when Judas and Silas were with the church they said "much to encourage and strengthen the brothers".

So as you read this book I believe that God wants to awaken hope again. He wants to breathe on your dreams and on what you thought had died and bring new clarity! He wants you to take time to sit in a prophetic atmosphere and be encouraged and take hope! At the moment you may identify with Ezekiel in the following scripture:

> *Then he said to me: "Son of man, these bones are the whole house of Israel. They say, 'Our bones are dried up and our hope is gone; we are cut off.'"*
>
> Ezekiel 37:11

But God has a promise for you. This is the time to prophesy to the dry bones of disappointment; it is the time to speak to the land that has seemed so barren and awaken what seems to have died. This is not the declaration of positive thinking, or speaking mere fantasies, but this hope that will grow is rooted in the words of revelation over your life. These are the very creative words of God and as he has spoken, so he will do it. So watch and see: the days of birthing your dreams are coming!

CHAPTER 8

Prophetic Prayer – Sounding Like Heaven When I Pray!

There is nothing more thrilling than praying and then watching your prayer being answered quickly! I was sent this testimony about answered prayer, so read and enjoy:

During the conference Rachel was speaking. Afterwards she offered to pray for those who had physical sickness and had several words of knowledge. The line was long and I saw many who seemed to be needier than I, so I hesitated but decided to hang back in the line and pray for Rachel. Time was running out and Rachel had to be somewhere else. So she asked those still standing in the line to make a semi-circle and said that she would quickly go by and lay hands on each of us and pray. She then went around touching each one on the forehead... but when she came to me she put her hand on the right side of my chest and then the left. Little did she know that the day before I was diagnosed with 85 per cent invasive breast cancer. Five weeks later I was completely healed, much to the surprise of the medical world. Thank you Rachel for being obedient in the quickness of the moment and for the slight touch of your fingers. Our God is the greatest in the little moment.

Ruth, Portland, Oregon

In these days God is teaching his church to pray in agreement with his heart. This means that the language of our prayer changes. We no longer come to God with pleading petitions hoping that he will hear us, but rather we can come knowing that we have already heard him speak, so we can pray boldly. We need to be a listening church, not just a talking one!

WHAT IS PROPHETIC PRAYER?

There are many types of prayer but what are the specific characteristics of prophetic prayer? Prophetic prayer is where you have an urge, prompted by the Holy Spirit, to pray for a situation about which you can have very little natural knowledge. You find you pray the requests of God. He prompts you to pray so that you can intervene and stand in the gap with his Word. This type of prayer depends upon good two-way communication between yourself and God. This is where you hear the heart of God by revelation and then you speak back to God about the situation in prayer. Prophetic prayer is not the prayer triggered on earth by the lists of people's needs and circumstances, but this prayer is prompted by revelation from heaven which focuses your prayer towards a particular issue. This type of prayer requires you to listen to God before you pray. You need to take time to wait, listen, then speak. For example, you may feel that you need to pray for the nations. First take some time and ask God which nation, and then ask which particular area of the nation – should it be a geographical area or the government?

Then, as you begin to pray, you find that God will often remind you of prophetic words or scriptures concerning the situation. I remember when I first returned to the UK in 1990, I often found myself praying Isaiah 60:1–3 over the nation. I felt God say that this scripture, "Arise and shine", was a declaration calling forth his glory over our nation. God wanted us to arise and be glory carriers who would release light into all the darkness in the land! Prophetic prayer often has strong authoritative declaration, as you are calling God's Word into the situation, not just praying your ideas. A prophetic prayer is a flowing forth of his Word through your spirit for a specific situation. So this prayer is letting God's desires be spoken through my mouth. His Word is not weak and pathetic, so it often sounds passionate!

LISTENING EARS

Good listening is so much part of good praying. However, as we have already discussed, a calloused heart does affect your hearing. But limited spiritual hearing will also restrict your faith, as your ability to believe and hear is linked in the Spirit. In Romans 10:17–18 we read:

> Consequently, faith comes from hearing the message, and the message is heard through the word of Christ. But I ask: Did they not hear?

So we need to let God soften our hearts towards the community, then allow him to open our ears to their cry, and then teach us to have faith for breakthrough in the lives of our friends and neighbours as we pray. We need the oil of the Holy Spirit to lubricate our ears so that we can hear the voice of God distinctly.

In 1986 we were working in Blantyre, Malawi, with Reinhard Bonnke and the Christ for All Nations team preparing for a Crusade, and I want to share with you the remarkable story of a beggar man who used to sit at the bottom of the stairs to our office. He was a cripple, paralysed from his hips downwards, and he used to move by dragging himself along the pavements with his arms. Despite his disability he was often smiling even though it was obvious he had a hard life. Once the meetings started we asked him if he would like to come with us and hear about Jesus. He agreed and so we took him in our vehicle. That night he received prayer and the power of God went through his body: his legs, usually stone cold, became warm and he began to have feeling in his feet again. However, when he tried to walk he could not. Disappointed, he returned home and was back at the bottom of our stairs begging later that week. Certain that this man had had a healing encounter with God, I decided to pray about his situation. The next day a pastor from one of the local churches came to me and said, "I have been praying for your beggar and feel that we need to anoint him with oil for one year." She went on to explain: "This man's limbs are so calloused from being dragged along on the roads that they cannot move because the skin is too hard, but I believe if we will soak his legs in warm oil and massage him every day, he will walk again. We just need to remove all the dead skin and then he will walk!" So this is what they did, long after we had to leave Blantyre for the next mission: this congregation came and massaged this man with oil for one year.

When I returned to Malawi ten years later I was walking in the market when I heard my name being shouted: "Mama Rachel, Bonnke Lady, Mama Rachel, please stop!" So I stopped and turned around to see a strong man running towards me. "I am your beggar man," he said, "but now my name is Abraham. I am an evangelist and I share the news of Jesus everywhere." He then told me how after being massaged with warm oil, his legs had begun to move more and more until all the dead, hardened skin was removed, and now he could walk perfectly.

In the same way, I believe God wants to unblock our ears and lubricate them with his warm oil, removing all the hardened areas of our heart so that we can arise and walk as a church of faith in this hour. For too long our faith and hearing have been crippled, but God has come to heal us and enable us to walk as children of faith with soft hearts and sensitive hearing. So, church, let us surrender our lives to this warm oil of his Spirit and be healed! We need to be a listening church so that we can pray the effective prayers of faith from the heart of our Father.

CRIES OF PROPHETIC INTERCESSION

As we begin to pray with these listening ears, we will hear the cry of the heart of God. All over the world at this time you will find that people are hearing these same words: "Deliverance, Harvest time, Community, and Government", plus many others. These are the prophetic cries in the Spirit that God wants us to understand as his church. Prophetic intercession is the process which enables us to partner spiritually with God. As we understand these prophetic calls, our spirit becomes attuned to the purpose of God so that we can recognize what he is doing and work with him more effectively. We need to be like Jesus, those who can truly say, "All that I do only reflects what I see my Father doing in heaven." So let us understand these prophetic cries of intercession that God is releasing through the church at this time.

THE PROPHETIC CRY FOR DELIVERANCE

God wants us to stand with the captives and shout "Freedom!" All around us we can see those who are trapped by addictions, compulsive sin and misery. People are held by the devil and the church needs to find her authority in the place of prayer and begin to declare freedom to the slaves. In Jeremiah 30:6–8 we read:

> Ask and see: Can a man bear children? Then why do I see every strong man with his hands on his stomach like a woman in labour, every face turned deathly pale? How awful that day will be! None will be like it. It will be a time of trouble for Jacob, but he will be saved out of it. "In that day," declares the Lord Almighty, "I will break the yoke off their necks and will tear off their bonds; no longer will foreigners enslave them."

Here we see that desperate times require desperate measures! There is such trouble in the land that the men experience "spiritual birth pains" as they labour in prayer for the freedom of the people. I believe that just as God heard the cry of suffering and was concerned for the Israelites in the book of Exodus, so God hears the groaning of the people under a heavy yoke of slavery today. So he calls us to partner with his concerns and cry out for the deliverance of the burdened. There is so much hopelessness and pain all around us; but it is our privilege to hear this cry and break the yokes of their spiritual oppression in prayer. So let us cry "Freedom!" and watch God set the captives free!

THE PROPHETIC CRY FOR HARVEST

"In that day I will restore David's fallen tent. I will repair its broken places, restore its ruins, and build it as it used to be, so that they may possess the remnant of Edom and all the nations that bear my name," declares the Lord, who will do these things. "The days are coming," declares the Lord, "when the reaper will be overtaken by the ploughman and the planter by the one treading grapes. New wine will drip from the mountains and flow from all the hills."

Amos 9:11–13

When Scripture uses the phrase, "in that day" or "in the fullness of time", we need to recognize that these phrases denote an encounter moment when *chronos*, the time on earth, aligns with *kairos*, the eternal time of heaven, and God breaks through! So here the prophet Amos is speaking about one of these expected instances. On "that day" there will be a rapid harvest and a restoration of the church and we will see an acceleration of fruitfulness in all our work. Suddenly we will find that we will be reaping the harvest faster than we can sow the seed. We will see the legacy and investment of past prayers and promises flourish and it will be a time to touch and see the reality of our hope materializing! What a wonderful day! But at the moment we are not living in the "that day" time span, so we still need to live in the "this" day of pre-harvest, and these days demand hard work. We need to work in the season of tears before the joy; we need to labour in the days of sowing before reaping. So this is the season to release the prophetic cry for harvest, crying out for change in our generation, government and society, knowing that God has promised to visit us.

THE PROPHETIC CRY FOR RIGHTEOUSNESS WITH JUSTICE

All through society at the moment we can observe the confusion of administering justice without understanding righteousness. We read of prison sentences that appear to favour the villain rather than the victim and wonder why. But here we must recognize the challenge that true righteousness and justice can only work together intelligently when God defines the "right" standard! Today our concept of "righteousness" encompasses the attitudes of virtue, morality, uprightness, honesty and decency. But "righteousness" in the original text denotes far more than this everyday use; indeed, true biblical righteousness is generally at odds with our current usage. We generally understand righteousness to mean "uprightness" in the sense of "adherence or conformity to an established norm", but the biblical usage of righteousness is rooted in covenants and relationships.

A simple definition of righteousness for us as Christians today is: the actions and attitudes that maintain us in a right relationship with God. True righteousness is rooted in the deep sense of right and wrong; it needs boundaries of absolute truth defined by God and then requires that we make right choices.

How we need this cry for righteousness in the land! But if we want to experience good biblical government, we need to see more than just righteousness in our governments – we need to see both justice and righteousness partner together.

Justice portrays an image of fairness, impartiality and even-handedness, and has two major aspects. Firstly, it is the standard by which penalties are given for breaking the requirements of society and secondly, it is the standard by which the advantages of social life are handed out, including material goods such as homes, clothes and food, and the rights of citizenship, job opportunities, and other liberties. As love is the central theme for the New Testament, so justice is the central ethical idea in the Old. Justice has a strong need to express compassion. It carries a heart for the marginalized and those of poorer and socially disadvantaged families. It wants their cry to be heard in the land.

THE PROPHETIC CRY FOR GOVERNMENT

As we pray for our government and cry out for Godly legislation, we need to understand this partnership. All through Scripture we see that we can only experience biblical government if we see righteousness and justice working together. You must have both. Here are just some of the numerous scriptures showing the biblical government of justice and righteousness:

> *The Almighty is beyond our reach and exalted in power; in his justice and great righteousness, he does not oppress.*
>
> Job 37:23

Righteousness and justice are the foundation of your throne; love and faithfulness go before you.

Psalm 89:14

Of the increase of his government and peace there will be no end. He will reign on David's throne and over his kingdom, establishing and upholding it with justice and righteousness from that time on and forever. The zeal of the Lord Almighty will accomplish this.

Isaiah 9:7

In love a throne will be established; in faithfulness a man will sit on it – one from the house of David – one who in judging seeks justice and speeds the cause of righteousness.

Isaiah 16:5

So as we pray for our government during elections and cry out for our leaders, we must understand we will never have true Christian policies until we have this combination. Too often we have governments with huge social programmes but no standards and boundaries for lifestyle, or policies that define tight legal boundaries but then have no compassion towards the one caught in the middle of the rules. Until we get true biblical attitudes in politics, we will always have compromise in our governments. Most political decisions seem to choose between righteousness and justice but no party or government seems to build on both these foundations! So we need to cry out:

Lift up your heads, O you gates; be lifted up, you ancient doors, that the King of glory may come in. Who is this King of glory? The Lord strong and mighty, the Lord mighty in battle. Lift up your heads, O you gates; lift them up, you ancient doors, that the King of glory may come in.

Psalm 24:7–9

We need to pray that the "gates", the places of authority in our communities, will allow this new legacy of government into their midst. We need to release a prophetic cry from the church that we want to see righteous authority balanced with justice sitting in the gates of Finance, Commerce, Education, Social Culture, Health, the Media and so on. We want to see God's kingdom come!

We need to release a prophetic cry for the marginalized, for God is hearing their cries of distress from injustice in our land. In these two scriptures we see the priority that God gives to the justice issues in our land and we need to echo his cry:

Do not mistreat an alien or oppress him, for you were aliens in Egypt. Do not take advantage of a widow or an orphan. If you do and they cry out to me, I will certainly hear their cry.

Exodus 22:21–23

Then you will call, and the Lord will answer; you will cry for help, and he will say: Here am I. "If you do away with the yoke of oppression, with the pointing finger and malicious talk, and if you spend yourselves on behalf of the hungry and satisfy the needs of the oppressed, then your light will rise in the darkness, and your night will become like the noonday."

Isaiah 58:9–10

So let us be those who hear his cry and serve the hurting and stand without compromise for the truth of God. It is so much easier to speak out against injustice than it is to be a voice for righteousness, but we need to be the sound for both!

THE PROPHETIC CRY FOR MERCY

You may wonder why we should pray for nations and governments. Surely God has decided what he will do, so does it make any difference? But if we examine the lives of the prophets, we find that all of them were intercessors for their nations in times of crisis. We are familiar with the famous prophetic cry of Habakkuk, "Oh God, in wrath remember mercy!" We read that Daniel fasted and prayed for his nation for twenty-one days, engaging in an intense spiritual battle. We also know the story of Jonah sent on assignment as a prophet to the great city of Nineveh, where he was told to preach against it, because its wickedness had come to the attention of God. After some reluctance Jonah did go and deliver his message of judgment, but the people's response was not what Jonah expected. They responded in humility as follows:

> "Who knows? God may yet relent and with compassion turn from his fierce anger so that we will not perish." When God saw what they did and how they turned from their evil ways, he had compassion and did not bring upon them the destruction he had threatened.
>
> Jonah 3:9–10

So why do I believe that we should pray and release these prophetic cries of intercession? Can we change the mind of

God? I believe that when God says he is coming to a nation, city or person, then God comes and keeps his word, but just as we read here concerning the city of Nineveh, I believe we can determine *the way in which he comes* through our prayers! Will God come in mercy or judgment? God has promised us that he who is coming will come, so we had better get ready! We will not be able to alter the timing of God but I do believe he will hear our cry and may adjust the way in which he comes to visit us if we will cry out!

So let us cry out for our nations. Surely as we look around us we can see the godlessness. We deserve the wrath of God, but let us touch heaven with a cry of mercy and watch what our God will do for us!

CHAPTER 9

Prophetic Song and the Psalmist

As we learn to listen and release the cry of God, we also find we become sensitive to the different sounds of his voice. Sometimes the voice of God sounds like thunder, as we read in this marvellous passage:

> Listen! Listen to the roar of his voice, to the rumbling that comes from his mouth. He unleashes his lightning beneath the whole heaven and sends it to the ends of the earth. After that comes the sound of his roar; he thunders with his majestic voice. When his voice resounds, he holds nothing back. God's voice thunders in marvellous ways; he does great things beyond our understanding.
>
> Job 37:2–5

However, others describe the voice of God as still and quiet. So when learning to hear the voice of God, we need to understand his ways and how he uses sound to communicate his heart. God is not limited to just speaking his Word in a written context or a spoken word, but he uses many mediums of communication. He speaks through creation and landscapes; beauty and colour; music and art too. In these days the church is rediscovering its ability to hear God through creative arts and music, and this is so much part of prophetic communication.

DISCOVERING THE SINGING GOD

Music has a heavenly dynamic, and is a part of creation that proceeds from the very personality of God himself. Unfortunately so much of our popular music today has lost its God-centred sound and so we have been tempted to see music as essentially evil. But our God loves and creates music – he is a singing God! He loves to sing over us and communicate to us through song, as we read here:

> *The Lord your God is with you, he is mighty to save. He will take great delight in you, he will quiet you with his love, he will rejoice over you with singing.*
>
> Zephaniah 3:17

God has a powerful voice, and we read in the book of Revelation that Jesus, the Lamb, will sing the "Song of the Lamb" in heaven, and the Holy Spirit inspires songs and melodies. The whole Trinity is musical! Then you will notice that the longest book of the Bible, Psalms, is a complete book of songs! Scripture shows us that music existed in heaven and with the angelic realm before the earth was even created. So music is part of God's world!

STARTING MY SINGING LESSONS WITH GOD

I love this challenge that we read in the book of Job:

> *Where were you when I laid the earth's foundation...*
> *while the morning stars sang together and all the*
> *angels shouted for joy?*
>
> Job 38:4, 7

You can just hear God provoking us to take our place with the rest of creation and start making a noise. If the stars sing together each morning and the angels are shouting with joy, then we had better take our place and learn our musical sound. As Spirit-filled Christians we are instructed to sing psalms, hymns and spiritual songs (Ephesians 5:19). We know that music has the power to move the inner affections of the heart and so Satan has perverted this power to capture and influence many people. This power of communication through music was created to be used to honour God and celebrate him. But we also need to recognize that God still speaks through music and wants to release modern-day psalmists who sing the prophetic song of the Lord and who are able to inspire the church.

THE PROPHETIC SONG

A prophetic song is when a person, prophetically inspired, is led to sing a song that they have not previously written, expressing the heart of God towards his people. The lyrics and the music of the song come by revelation and then the person expresses the sound and sense that they hear in their spirit. Here we are mixing the atmosphere of music with the Spirit of revelation to release the Word of God. The use of music should enhance the ability of the people to sense the presence of God and hear his Word. Although the actual singing of the prophetic song will often be spontaneous during a time of worship, it is important that the musicians and prophetic people take time to learn to work together. We should not be surprised when the prophetic is released during a time of worship, as Jesus loves to be in the midst of praise and he is the Spirit of prophecy. So if we are to develop a new generation of prophetic psalmists, we need to cultivate a musical environment where it is easy to hear the voice of God and then listen. There is nothing better than worshipping and finding that heaven has opened and people are getting touched and healed in this prophetic atmosphere of worship. So read this testimony from Scotland:

> We just wanted to let you know that God has answered our prayers and that your prophecy about us becoming parents in the natural has come to pass!! Our precious Noah was born on the 4th of May 2008. We called him Noah because we can testify that God is faithful to His promises. It continued to be a long journey after your prophetic word in 2006 but we held onto it the best we could. In fact God took us to a place of deep surrender and peace in spring/summer 2007 and spoke to us both separately about letting go and rising up like eagles and learning to worship Him as fully and wholeheartedly as we could. This we did and it was a wonderful time for us – Noah was conceived out of this. We felt God's favour was released as we worshipped and Noah came into being. Praise God!
> With Love in Him,
> Paul, Jan & Noah B.

MODERN-DAY PSALMISTS

So what is a modern-day psalmist or prophetic minstrel? I believe that these are people who have an established prophetic ministry that is often expressed through music or song. They are key worship leaders, who also carry a strong prophetic anointing with their musical gifting and usually move at a national or international level. They often write songs that express the heart of God for the church prophetically or write about the issues of the day, prophesying through their songs. Not all worship leaders will be psalmists, but some are. Often it is difficult to decide whether these people are gifted musicians who also carry a mature prophetic ministry or prophets who are also brilliant musicians!

LET OUR MUSIC RELEASE THE PROPHETS

Good music will stimulate the prophetic gift in the church. We notice that when Elisha wanted to prophesy he asked that someone bring him a harpist. In 2 Kings 3 we read that while the harpist was playing, the hand of the Lord came upon Elisha and then he was able to speak and began to prophesy and say, "This is what the Lord says…!" We can learn a lesson here and need to appreciate that we can create atmospheres that are more conducive to hearing the voice of God. In the right musical environment you can feel the hand of the Lord come upon you as you are in his presence and then know the Word of the Lord being released through you as you speak. The Spirit of prophecy came upon Elisha as the harp was being played. So let us also cultivate an ambience where the hand of the Lord comes upon people and then the Word comes through them with power.

CULTIVATING AN ATMOSPHERE FOR PROPHETIC WORSHIP

So you want to develop prophetic worship in your church? Well, this is both a learnt skill and a spontaneous happening. It requires sensitive cooperation between the worship leader, the musicians, other leaders and the congregation. The musicians need to learn that they cannot expect to adhere to their scripted plan and music sheets each time they play, but they need to be flexible to changes in rhythms, keys and song orders in order to fit with what the leader senses God is doing. As the leader you need to be prepared to call forth certain sounds or rhythms by selecting certain musicians to play their instrument or singers to prophesy. You need to ask God to give you wisdom to generate a prophetic atmosphere by releasing the instruments to demonstrate the sound of the heart of God. For example, if you are sensing that God wants to speak about his love for the broken, you may ask a violinist to play a solo piece prophetically, just expressing this heart of God. Usually this musician would not follow a musical script but would just improvise and play the music that they sense in their spirit. You need to encourage your musicians to practise playing without a music score so that they feel confident to just play the free flow of the music that they sense.

Like a spiritual conductor, train your musicians to be aware of the different instruments playing with them so that if you recognize there is an anointing on one sound, they will let that instrument play alone and express this prophetic sound. I have been in a meeting where all the instruments paused, allowing the saxophone to continue playing alone in a minor key, and the sound just made people weep as they sensed the heart of God for the lonely. As the leader you need to be aware of the rhythm and beat of the song. A simple rhythm change can release a spirit of dancing necessary for breakthrough. Sometimes I watch good musicians hold the pace of the music to the correct rhythm and, although technically correct, it kills the spirit of joy longing to be released by the congregation. So allow the speed of a song to accelerate, if you sense there is a prophetic momentum that needs to be released so that people can dance, even though this is not musically correct! Then at the end of the song do not end with definite, hard chords but keep a gentle flow of music playing so that if someone has a prophetic song, they are able to flow into the space at the end of this song. It is often good to leave some spaces for improvised playing as you transition between the planned songs, as this encourages those with prophetic songs to find a space and courage to sing out. So let us be leaders like Paul, who encouraged his congregations to participate:

> *What then shall we say, brothers? When you come together, everyone has a hymn, or a word of instruction, a revelation, a tongue or an interpretation. All of these must be done for the strengthening of the church.*
>
> 1 Corinthians 14:26

Finally, we need to make sure we have an attitude that welcomes the prophetic sound in our worship. Sometimes musicians or worship leaders can view the prophetic songs and contributions as an unwelcome interruption to their planned worship slot. But this sense of irritation can be justified if there are endless contributions that are poor in content and musical ability. So in order to deal with these tensions that could grow concerning the prophetic, you need to have a good prophetic protocol in place so that both the worship team and the congregation understand how and when they should contribute and what is appropriate (refer to Chapter 6 on prophetic protocol). Prophetic worship should not become a time when anything is allowed to happen because it is "prophetic"! But rather we need to work together and create an atmosphere where the music and spiritual songs strengthen people so that they leave our services knowing that they have connected with God and have been touched by his presence.

DEVELOPING THE PROPHETIC SONG

Below are seven practical steps that I believe will help you develop this side of your prophetic gift:

Practise in private

Take time to sing during your private devotional time. Just sing what is in your heart and learn to recognize the prophetic anointing and how to flow with it musically. Many of us will never sing publicly, thank goodness, so enjoy making a joyful noise in private.

Start small and safe

If God then begins to challenge you to sing out spontaneously in a public place, choose safe settings when you start. Take the risk and sing out in a smaller group. Afterwards ask your friends and leaders to give you feedback about the content and style, and be willing to learn and be corrected if necessary. Home groups or worship practice nights are ideal places to experiment and learn.

Sing out in a church meeting

Initially it is wiser to sing a song revealing our heart of worship towards God and then progress later to expressing his heart for the people. Learn to work with your worship team and make sure you have a relationship with them so that they understand how you like to sing and can support you appropriately with the right key or rhythm. You need to sense the specific heart-cry of God in that meeting and then express it as a spontaneous and inspirational song – for example, a cry for mercy, a lament for sin, a celebration of joy and so on.

Use the Bible

At home, practise by memorizing and using Scripture to give you themes and words. Then you will find that you can draw on these phrases and sing them prophetically. Often the book of Psalms is a good resource for inspirational material. If you immerse yourself in Scripture, your songs will be richer, and there will be a richer depth to the content. Remember, God's Word is already anointed!

Do not limit yourself to just spontaneous songs

As you spend time with God in the secret place, he will give you prophetic and inspirational songs that you can write down and keep for yourself. Sometimes you may find that God then reminds you of this song at a particular time months later and then you sing it publicly. At other times God can remind you of an old hymn or other songs, but suddenly, under the creative leadership of the Holy Spirit, they will carry a fresh relevance and prophetic edge and usher in the presence of God. So be sensitive and sing what he gives you.

Don't be too concerned if you make a musical mess!

It does not matter if you miss a note or confuse your rhythm once or twice. Do not worry: just because you make a mistake does not mean that the content of your word was incorrect! But if you do tend to sing out of tune as a rule, maybe speaking the word is a better medium for you, as someone shrieking off-key can really distract people from hearing the message!

Let your song have a clear and simple message

It needs to be a prophetic call with a distinct message! It should not be too mystical in content and should only contain a directional element if this has already been agreed by the leaders. Here the same protocol guidelines as those for the spoken prophetic words should apply to content and delivery style (detailed in Chapter 6).

RELIEF FROM TORMENTING SPIRITS

When I moved to Oxford I was surprised at the number of needy people that I saw walking through the city centre. I realized that so many of these people had suffered from addictions to alcohol or drugs and were now tormented by evil spirits that wanted to rob them of their sanity. As we began to learn their names they started to come to our church services. When we asked them about their reasons for coming to church, they would frequently reply, "Well, I just get a good vibe when I'm here", "It's good and you can think straight", "It's real peaceful, ain't it?", "You get a buzz – you get a kick", "I like the happy faces" – and many other replies. But we discovered that the presence of God provides a place of refuge for those who are being tormented.

In 1 Samuel 16:16–18, 23 we read the story of how Saul was advised to use spiritual music to pacify him when he was being tormented:

> "Let our lord command his servants here to search for someone who can play the harp. He will play when the evil spirit from God comes upon you, and you will feel better." So Saul said to his attendants, "Find someone who plays well and bring him to me." One of the servants answered, "I have seen a son of Jesse of Bethlehem who knows how to play the harp. He is a brave man and a warrior. He speaks well and is a fine-looking man. And the Lord is with him"... Whenever the spirit from God came upon Saul, David would take his harp and play. Then relief would come to Saul; he would feel better, and the evil spirit would leave him.

Here we see that David is recommended to come and play not only because of his musical talent but also because of his character. The servant had noted that not only did David play well but he also spoke well and was known to carry the presence of God! So David was hired to play and release a prophetic sound that would bring comfort to the troubled King Saul. In verse 23 we read that as David played, relief would come to Saul. The Hebrew word *ruwach* is translated as "relief" here in this version, but this word has a more profound meaning – to breathe freely, to revive, to give ample room, to be refreshed, to enlarge. So David's prophetic playing of the harp suppressed the demonic authority in Saul's life and brought peace and relief as the music breathed into his spiritual man and revived him. So now we can understand why people often say after a good worship time, "I feel different – I feel I have some space now, I feel refreshed!"

They have just experienced the "relief" of God.

SONGS OF DELIVERANCE

Finally, as we sing let us create a firewall of protection around the lives of the people that we know and protect them from every work of the enemy. I love this promise in Psalm 32:7:

You are my hiding place; you will protect me from trouble and surround me with songs of deliverance.

I have often observed, as people sing or musicians play their prophetic word over someone, how they are then released from their fears or sickness. As we sing, our sound of praise and worship brings confusion to the enemy, and then calls forth victory! This song of the Lord prophesies into the face of the enemy, worships God and declares the truth on earth! When we worship in this way we need to have a three-dimensional view of the effect of our worship, as we are indeed touching heaven, changing lives and rebuking the enemy! We are not just "singing to God" but we are making prophetic declarations into the heavens above and the earth beneath, and you will find that these words have power to alter history!

When we were in Malaysia there was a prayer group in Penang who had a heart for their city. One day they were horrified when they discovered that a huge new idol was being built right on their patch. So they decided they would fast and pray. After a few days one of the girls sensed the Holy Spirit asking them to go down to the temple area as a group and spend some time worshipping outside the gate for seven days. So they did this for one week and went home. Imagine their surprise when the local newspaper announced the next day that the temple idol had developed severe structural cracks and so was to be closed to all visitors. After six months of surveys and examinations it was then decided that the faults could not be repaired and the temple would have to close!

So surround the enemy with these violent songs of deliverance! Let God fill our mouths with a sound that resonates and brings breakthrough. This is the time for the church to arise with songs of deliverance. As we spend time understanding and studying the Word of God, we will become those who declare it more effectively. God has given us this weapon, his Word, the sword of the Spirit, so let us become skilled warriors and watch this Word do its work in lives all around us!

CHAPTER 10

Let the Word Do Its Work!

My Dad loves his Bible. In fact if you turn to the dedication at the beginning of this book you will find that I have thanked him. But if he were to tell you his story, you would discover that it was not always that way! As a young boy he was taken to Sunday school at his local Baptist church but once he entered his teenage years he decided that this "religion stuff" was not for him. He was a keen rugby player with a sharp scientific mind and there was no room for God in this mix. But Dad had a praying grandmother, who had been part of the Welsh Revival in 1904, and she would send him a Bible each year for his Christmas gift. However, Dad did not appreciate this and usually destroyed it in various ways, wanting the Bible out of his life. Dad then fell in love, married my Mum, who was only nineteen, began working for Kodak as a research scientist, and quickly climbed the career ladder. He was successful and admired by his colleagues, happy with his new wife, and dreaming of a lavish life in America. Mum soon got pregnant with their first child and gave birth to a son, who then tragically died a few days after birth. Mum, who had a Methodist background, wanted comfort, began to think about God, and rediscovered her old Bible in the attic, but Dad was still a determined atheist and would give God no part in his life.

But suddenly this all changed! Unwittingly some Mormon missionaries helped my father find Jesus. "How?" you ask. Well, it was the power of the Word! One day, when he was still dreaming of America, the doorbell rang and Dad opened the door to find two American boys on the doorstep. So Dad made a deal with them. They could come round to his home each week for two hours, but they were only allowed to talk about their religion for one hour, and then Dad would ask them questions about the USA for the second hour. But as soon as these Mormons began to talk about the Bible, Dad's research mind was triggered. He quickly deduced that what they were expressing was different to what he had been taught in Sunday school and so he decided to find a Bible to check this out. He thought he would debate with these lads, making this first hour's discussion more stimulating, and showing these "poor" boys that their religion was useless. So, he found a Bible and began to read. Soon he was captivated, challenged and curious. He realized the Bible was an incredible book. Finally he made a decision: that if God was the person that he described himself to be in this book, then he was worth everything; but if he fell short of this person, God was the biggest fraud out there. The Word had infiltrated my Dad's life, and he was ruined! So he prayed a strange prayer: "God, if you are the God of this book, show yourself to me in the next three months and I will give you my life forever; but if you do not reveal yourself to me, or if you show me that you are not like the God in this Bible, then I will never give you the time of day again!" Well, my Dad discovered that the God of this Bible was real in a few days, and soon both my parents were passionate lovers of Jesus, totally changed by reading the Bible!

My transformed parents were soon on a ship for Bombay, India, where my Dad spent his early missionary years printing Bibles with the Gospel Literature Service Press. Dad, who had once destroyed and burnt this precious book, was now printing Bibles in the thousands for the Indian people! Like the apostle Paul, Dad was changed and the things that he had hated and persecuted he now cherishes and loves with a deep affection. So I know that this Word has great power to do its work both in the lives of the broken and even the obstinate. The Word of God will win the day, so let this Word do its work!

My parents now live in America, fulfilling the dream of their early marriage, but only after serving God in many other nations first. Now it is our turn. Will we take this Word wherever God sends us? Will we take time to let the Word work in us and then speak through us? Today I have the privilege of continuing this generational line of preachers and teachers. I have chosen to be one who loves the Word of God and who then takes it to the nations.

BACK IN CHINA

So here I was, standing to preach in front of these precious brothers and sisters in China. As I looked at their faces I was deeply humbled. I knew that they were eagerly expecting a word from God. Many of them had experienced persecution and prison, moved in mighty miracles and even seen the dead raised. They were hearers and doers of this Word that they so respected, but they still wanted more! As I preached God's Word over these days, their capacity to listen and desire to learn more about the Bible deeply affected me. Many of them had already paid a price for their faith. In fact the reason the room was predominantly filled with women, was because many of the men were still serving prison sentences for being believers. The Bible was a precious gift to them and, like Mary Jones, many had paid an extreme price to own their own copy. During the Cultural Revolution in China, all ideological and religious works were banned except for a few chosen and approved works, notably Chairman Mao's *Red Book*. Most Chinese had grown up having never seen a Bible. Many possessed small portions of the Scriptures that they had painstakingly copied by hand; all those who had any part of the Bible risked imprisonment. But every Chinese believer that I have met has a burning passion to have, hold and preach the Word of God. To them, to own a "real" Bible is the greatest treasure! So enjoy the following story of one man's quest for a Bible in China.

Brother Yun, a brand-new Chinese Christian, was told by his mother that the only revelation of Jesus left to us on earth was in the Bible. So having just converted to Christ, it became Yun's sole passion to own a copy of his own. But as he enquired about this, he was told that very few people in China had access to a Bible for themselves. However, there was an elderly pastor living in a neighbouring village who was known to have his own copy. So Yun went to visit this pastor to buy a Bible or ask how he may obtain his own Bible, and was advised that if he really wanted a copy he needed to pray for one. The pastor told Yun, "The Bible is a heavenly book. If you want one, you'll need to pray to the God of heaven. Only he can provide you with a heavenly book." So, after praying for several weeks, Yun returned to the pastor, anxious and desperate, as he still had no Bible. So the pastor instructed him further, "You should not only kneel down and pray to the Lord, you should also fast and weep. The more you weep, the sooner you'll get a Bible."

So Yun fasted and prayed for 100 days until his parents were afraid he could lose his mind, such was his earnestness. But then, while sleeping, he suddenly had a vision of three men coming towards him with a big cart full of fresh bread. In the vision he went to beg for food for his family and one of the men asked him if he were hungry. He then took out a red bag and handed it to him. As Yun took out the bread and ate it, it turned into a Bible in his mouth and he knew he had been given the Word to satisfy his hunger. On awakening Yun searched his house looking for the Bible that had been given to him, as the vision had been so clear he thought it was real, but he found nothing. But very early that next morning there was a knock at the door and the man he had seen in the vision stood there and handed him a red bag with a Bible in it. He later discovered that an evangelist had also been given a vision with the exact location of Yun's house and this evangelist had been directed to take a Bible to a man in this house. Brother Yun treasured this gift and thanked God for his faithfulness. He then promised God that he would always devour the Word like a hungry child because he "fully trusted that the words in the Bible were God's words to me."

He then started to read his precious book, but it was more challenging to keep this promise than he initially realized. Having only had three years' formal education, Brother Yun struggled at first to read the Bible in this traditional Chinese script, but he persevered with the help of a dictionary. Once he had read through the whole Bible he then began to memorize it, one chapter each day. Later, when imprisoned for his faith, Yun recited these words of Scripture and the promises of God which he had stored in his heart, and it helped him survive times of extended torture and persecution. This treasured Word sustained him and gave him strength. Today he is a man who glows with the presence of Jesus, moves in the power of the Holy Spirit and still loves his Bible! He is a man who loves the Word and knows the Spirit.[1]

WORD AND SPIRIT

Smith Wigglesworth was famous for this quote:

> Never compare this Book with other books. This Book is from heaven. It does not contain the Word of God; it is the Word of God. It is supernatural in origin, eternal in duration and value, infinite in scope and divine in authorship. Read it through! Pray it in! Write it down. I am of course referring to the Bible.

Smith Wigglesworth was born on 8 June 1859, to a destitute family in Yorkshire, England. During his childhood he was illiterate. He grew up in a Methodist family, was confirmed by a Bishop into the Church of England, baptized by immersion in the Baptist Church and had a grounding in Bible teaching from the Plymouth Brethren while also doing an apprenticeship in the plumbing trade! Wigglesworth married Polly Featherstone in 1882. Polly was a gifted preacher with the Salvation Army. Polly then taught Smith to read the Bible and he often stated that it was the only book he had ever read. In 1907 Wigglesworth visited Alexander Boddy during the Sunderland Revival, and following a laying on of hands from Alexander's wife Mary, he experienced speaking in tongues and then worked with the Assemblies of God. Soon he gave up his plumbing trade as he was too busy preaching in the nations and seeing many healed, and even the dead were raised. He was a man known for loving the Word of God and moving in extraordinary power too.

It was said that Wigglesworth made a commitment to God that he would only sleep at night if he had won a soul for Christ that day. A story goes that on one occasion Wigglesworth could not sleep because he had not met this commitment, and so he got up and went back out into the night and there he met an alcoholic to whom he spoke and then persuaded to become a believer. Wigglesworth continued to minister right up until the time of his death on 12 March 1947. But shortly before Wigglesworth died, he gave a prophetic word to the church of Great Britain, instructing them to watch for various trends and especially to watch for the season when the Word and the Spirit would come together. Here is the prophecy attributed to Smith Wigglesworth in 1947:

> During the next few decades there will be two distinct moves of the Holy Spirit across the church in Great Britain. The first move will affect every church that is open to receive it, and will be characterized by a restoration of the baptism and gifts of the Holy Spirit.
>
> The second move of the Holy Spirit will result in people leaving historic churches and planting new churches.
>
> In the duration of each of these moves, the people who are involved will say, "This is a great revival." But the Lord says, "No, neither is this the great revival but both are steps towards it."
>
> When the new church phase is on the wane, there will be evidence in the churches of something that has not been seen before: a coming together of those with an emphasis on the Word and those with an emphasis on the Spirit. When the Word and the Spirit come together, there will be the biggest

> move of the Holy Spirit that the nation, and indeed the world, has ever seen. It will mark the beginning of a revival that will eclipse anything that has been witnessed within these shores, even the Wesleyan and Welsh revivals of former years. The outpouring of God's Spirit will flow over from the United Kingdom to mainland Europe, and from there, will begin a missionary move to the ends of the earth.

As you read these words today you can see that much of this word has already been fulfilled. We can observe all these trends in our recent church history. So now we must be entering the Word and the Spirit phase and we had better get ready for a wonderful move of God! Unfortunately, too often in the church we have had either a "Word" or a "Spirit" mentality. We pride ourselves that we are either a "Word-based" church or a "Spirit-led" one. Too often we have separated the Word from the Spirit, but now it is time for both: a church that is informed and biblically based, filled with people of revelation and the inspiration of the Spirit. This type of church will bring radical change in our society.

THE WONDER-WORKING POWER OF THE WORD

As we become disciplined people, committed to bringing change, we must remember that our job is just to release the Word. We cannot make anything happen. But the power is in the Word, so we must study it, equip ourselves with it and then declare it. Here is a wonderful testimony of a man who watched the power of the Bible literally change his life and his home!

On January 31, 1995, after 42 years of living for myself, God finally got my attention and I gave my life to Him; to His service. After belonging to my local church for six months, our senior pastor came to me and asked how I was doing my Bible reading. I told him that I was dyslexic and I had never read a book from cover to cover in my life. I had read some short stories in *Reader's Digest* or newspaper articles; things like that, but never a book. I, at this point in my life, had been married for 23 years and I have never taken care of my personal finances. My wife, Karen, had carried that burden the whole time. I would get twos and fives, threes and eights backwards. One mistake and we would be in trouble.

My pastor encouraged me to try to read the Bible in one year. I told him no. I can't do it. He answered me with Scripture, "you can do all things through Christ who strengthens you". He asked me again to try and said that before you start reading each day, pray, and ask God to renew your mind through the reading of the word. Again, he used scripture. I told him I would try. One year later I finished the Bible. I read it cover to cover and when I was finished my mind had been renewed and I was cured of dyslexia.

The pastor again encouraged me to continue on and to go to college. Start college at age 43? I enrolled in Christian Life School Theology. I went for two years and got my AA degree, then took a year off. I went back for another two years and got my Bachelor's Degree in Theology. I took over our family finances and was put in charge on the church's board of finances. At work they gave me my own budget and I oversee the running of a print shop for the State of Washington. My wife was then able to go to college and had gotten her AA degree and now our daughter is freshman at Portland Bible College in Portland, Oregon. God is wonderful. You really can do all things through Him. Praise the Lord forever and ever. Amen.

Mark and Karen, Portland, Oregon

Not only did the Bible change one life, it changed a family and then flowed down the generations! Today open your heart and believe that the Bible has the power to change you, your family and the generations to come. This is a new day! Unknown to Wigglesworth, his prophetic word still lives on with power, and now it is our honour to establish this word as we watch the Word and the Spirit come together. We have an opportunity to watch the power of God's Word work in our generation.

A CROSS ON THE ROAD

I was new to Oxford, we had only moved two weeks ago, and I was struggling to find my way through a crowd of wandering tourists. Feeling frustrated, I decided to cross over and walk down a back alley rather than this main street when I noticed a memorial in the middle of the road, and on closer inspection found this inscription:

To the Glory of God, and in grateful commemoration of His servants, Thomas Cranmer, Nicholas Ridley, Hugh Latimer, Prelates of the Church of England, who near this spot yielded their bodies to be burned, bearing witness to the sacred truths which they

had affirmed and maintained against the errors of
the Church of Rome, and rejoicing that to them it
was given not only to believe in Christ, but also to
suffer for His sake; this monument was erected
by public subscription in the year of our Lord God,
MDCCCXLI.

Suddenly my irritation with the crowded streets was gone; here
were real heroes who had paid the ultimate price for loving
the Bible. I discovered that the actual site of the execution
was close by, in Broad Street, located just outside the old city
walls. The site is still marked by a cross of cobbled stones sunk
into the tarmac road. As I looked at this cross in the road I
wondered if my life would leave a mark on the road of history
too. Would I leave a legacy of courage as I spoke the Word or
would I be silenced by intimidation?

A while ago I was returning home from a powerful
ministry trip. I had moved in words of revelation and
watched the preaching of the Word encourage many, and
then God asked me a question: "Rachel, how many in your
neighbourhood know that you carry the Word of God in your
life?" I felt the Holy Spirit challenge me further: "Rachel, if
you were to die, how many would come to your funeral from
your street because they have heard your Good News?" I
realized that it was not enough to preach powerfully where I
feel safe, but I must also carry this Word out onto the streets
and leave the mark of the cross wherever I go! I have decided
that I want my life also to leave a cross on the road. I want
to be a signpost that instructs people with words of life and
hope.

We have studied the heroes of our faith, both past and
present and now it is our turn to take the challenge. Will we
eat this Word and then speak it? Will we be those who carry

this treasure and help many to smell the aroma of the fresh bread of heaven? God is raising up a new prophetic generation who will speak with accuracy and power. Now is the time to arise and to discover the sound of God and release the voice of the church!

Notes

1. This true story is taken from Brother Yun and Paul Hattaway's *The Heavenly Man*, Oxford: Monarch Books, 2002, pp. 27–33.

Appendix:

PRAYER MINISTRY TEAMS IN THE LOCAL CHURCH

> *The Spirit of the Lord will rest on him – the Spirit of wisdom and of understanding, the Spirit of counsel and of power, the Spirit of knowledge and of the fear of the Lord – and he will delight in the fear of the Lord. He will not judge by what he sees with his eyes, or decide by what he hears with his ears; but with righteousness he will judge the needy, with justice he will give decisions for the poor of the earth.*
>
> Isaiah 11:2–4

Qualifications of prayer team members

Each team member should:

- Have the attitude of a servant and the heart of a shepherd.

- Be able to pray out loud with fluency and without embarrassment.

- Be full of the Holy Spirit and able to use the gifts.

- Have a good general knowledge and understanding of the Bible.

- Have a willingness to meet with others and be in accountable relationships within the local church.

Guidelines for developing prayer teams in the local church

- Have a trained prayer team ready to be on duty and to serve at all meetings.

- Remember to collect and use testimonies to encourage people that God is at work during prayer times.

- Destroy the idea that "only bad people need prayer" and cultivate an environment where people feel safe to ask for prayer.

- Remember that the people you pray for will be at different stages of understanding, so don't assume you know their level of maturity, their condition or their spiritual understanding.

- Pray for individuals as the Holy Spirit leads. Generally encourage the men to only pray for men and the women to only pray for women. But this is a principle, not a rule.

- Do not look for manifestations or dramatic results alone. If the person falls on the floor, make sure they are comfortable, modest and covered appropriately, and continue to pray even while they are on the floor if you still have a word for them. Ask God and the person what is happening before you move on to the next person.

- Work in pairs, with at least one person of the same sex as the person being prayed for. Learners should work with a more experienced team member.

- Discover the joy of partnership – always remember that you are partnering with the Holy Spirit who will equip and train you! So take time to listen and then speak. Ask the person if they understand any pictures or prophetic words that are given to them and be ready to explain them further so that there is no confusion.

How should we pray for the sick?

- With simple faith and confidence in the goodness of God. Encourage them to receive and believe with you. Take some time to talk and access the emotional and spiritual capacity of the person for whom you are going to pray.

- With love and compassion – use their name and be attentive to them. Do not lay a heavy hand on their body if they are in physical pain but be sensitive to their needs.

- Be aware that physical conditions can be (but are not always!) linked to emotional trauma, stress, issues of bitterness, unconfessed sin or unforgiveness. Is there anything to pray for here?

- Always give people permission to be real if nothing seems to be happening and never leave them feeling guilty or burdened. Encourage them to come back for prayer; sometimes healing is a process that takes time.

- Never accuse people of not having enough faith if they are not healed. We may not understand why people are not always instantly healed but it is OK to admit we don't know why!

- Try not to develop a rigid formula when praying for the sick. Do not look for particular manifestations in response to certain prayers. The Holy Spirit doesn't follow our rules!

- Don't be afraid of emotion in the person being prayed for. As they sense the presence of God they may become tearful, express anger or shout for joy!

- Always preserve the dignity of the person you are praying for. Be sensitive: only touch where it is appropriate or ask them to lay a hand on themselves and then put your hand on theirs.

- Never recommend or counsel someone to come off medication before they have been back to their doctor to have a full check-up.

A model for prayer

1. Ask the person's name and why they have come for prayer. Is it in response to something in the service/meeting? A particular need? Ask them, "What do you want Jesus to do for you?"

2. Assure people that they do not need to be afraid – it's a safe place, and encourage them to relax and connect with God; invite them to close their eyes and hold out their hands to signal receptivity and openness to God.

3. Invite the Holy Spirit to come; watch and wait; pray with your eyes open.

4. Pray as the Holy Spirit leads but don't be afraid of silence or silently praying in tongues.

5. You may wish to anoint them with oil as a sign of the Holy Spirit's presence and healing touch.

6. Ask if you can lay hands on their head or shoulder or the affected area if appropriate or, in more sensitive cases, get them to lay hands on themselves.

7. Pray simply and authoritatively in the name of Jesus.

8. Be open to words of knowledge.

9. After a while, stop and ask what's happening; gauge if you

need to keep praying or refer them for counselling or follow up. Don't take on more than you can handle and don't be afraid to ask for help from other, more experienced team members if you get stuck.

10. Share any insights.

11. Allow people to ask questions.

- If you have shared a prophetic word, then give people a chance to respond.

- Make sure people have understood what you mean if you have shared any impressions from God.

- Don't let them leave confused.

12. Bless them as they leave and debrief with the person overseeing the team if you feel at all uncomfortable or burdened, or you need to ensure the person is followed up.

13. We always seek to maintain a person's dignity and confidentiality, avoiding the temptation to gossip or use the information shared with us inappropriately. However, there are times when we ourselves need support or need to ensure there is appropriate ongoing follow-up, accountability or oversight. In this case it is always appropriate to inform the person that you will be sharing their situation with the team overseer or minister. If someone confesses child abuse you are legally obliged to report them and must tell them so.

How do we handle disappointment and "unanswered" prayer for healing?

So do not throw away your confidence; it will be richly rewarded. You need to persevere so that when you have done the will of God, you will receive what he has promised. For in just a very little while, "He who is coming will come and will not delay. But my righteous one will live by faith. And if he shrinks back, I will not be pleased with him." But we are not of those who shrink back and are destroyed, but of those who believe and are saved. Now faith is being sure of what we hope for and certain of what we do not see.

Hebrews 10:35–11:1

- Avoid glib, simplistic answers and don't look for someone to blame.

- Remember, bad things happen to good people.

- God is still God and he is still good – he doesn't change even if our circumstances do.

- Keep praying and don't be discouraged; always ask what the Father is doing.

- Remember the body, mind, soul connection and consider the person as a whole; ask God to reveal if there is anything more complex going on than a physical condition.

- Remember, healing is a battleground and sometimes we need to contend for it.

Areas for growth and application in your team

- Identify your strengths and weaknesses when praying for healing – where is your area of confidence? Which is the area in which you lack confidence?

- Find someone more experienced to begin to practise with and use the model above.

- Ask God to begin to give you words of knowledge concerning healing.

- Watch as God develops gifts in you. Do you have a gift of healing for a particular condition? Sometimes we will find we have faith for a specific condition and God begins to use us more in that area.

ABOUT THE AUTHOR

Rachel Hickson is an internationally respected prayer leader and Bible teacher with a recognized prophetic gift.

At the age of twenty-four Rachel, with her husband Gordon, worked alongside Reinhard Bonnke and the Christ for All Nations team in Africa. After just six weeks in Zimbabwe she almost lost her life in an horrific car accident, but was miraculously healed by God. This incident birthed in Rachel a desire to pray and to train others to realize the full potential of a praying church.

After returning from Africa in 1990, Rachel and Gordon pastored a group of four churches in the Hertfordshire area, and it was during this time that Heartcry Ministries was established, with a vision to equip and train people into their destiny within the church and the community.

In 2005 Rachel and Gordon moved to Oxford where Gordon is Associate Minister on the staff of St Aldates Church.

Rachel travels internationally, visiting Europe, North America, Africa and India. Invitations come from various denominational backgrounds, where a passion for unity has brought the churches together to pray for a move of God in their area. Rachel and Gordon have a passion to see cities transformed through the power of prayer and evangelism. One of their projects links churches and prayer ministries across London and has developed into a city strategy called the London Prayernet (see www.londonprayer.net).

Rachel has been married to Gordon for over twenty-nine years and they have two children. Nicola, their daughter, is married to Tim Douglass and they live in Sydney with their daughter, Leila. Rachel and Gordon's son, David, has just completed university and lives in the UK.

ABOUT HEARTCRY MINISTRIES

We work with churches and people from many nations and denominations to equip them in the following areas:

- *Prayer:* Training an army of ordinary people in Prayer Schools and seminars to become confident to break the sound barrier and pray informed, intelligent and passionate prayers.

- *Prophetic:* Equipping the church to be an accurate prophetic voice in the nation by teaching in training schools and conferences the principles of the prophetic gift. We seek to train people who are passionate to know the presence of God, are available to hear his voice and then learn to speak his Word with accuracy so that lives can be touched and changed.

- *Women:* Delivering a message of hope to women across the nations and cultures to help them arise with a new confidence so that they can be equipped and ready to fulfil their destiny and execute their kingdom purpose.

- *Capital cities:* Standing in the capital cities of the world, working with government institutions, business and the church, and then crying out for a new alignment of the natural and spiritual government in these places. A cry for London and beyond.

- *Business and finance:* Connecting business people with their kingdom purpose so that provision can partner more effectively with vision and accelerate the purpose of God in nations. Connecting commerce, community and church for change!

- *Leaders of tomorrow:* Mentoring and encouraging younger leaders to pioneer the next move of God in the areas of politics and government, social action and justice issues, creative arts and the media, and the ministry.

- *Nations:* Partnering with nations in Africa, the Middle East and India by supplying teaching, training and practical resources to strengthen and resource them as they work for breakthrough in their nations.

- *Media, TV and satellite:* Developing training materials to equip and disciple the church in the nations to understand and fulfil their responsibility. Being a voice of encouragement through TV into the homes of the army of ordinary people praying for impossible situations.

- *Resources and conferences:* Writing books, manuals and training materials that will equip the church to be prepared. Providing conferences and training days where leaders and the church can be encouraged to continue in their purpose and calling.

Heartcry hopes to continue strengthening the church to connect with its community whilst encouraging the people to hear the urgent call to prayer. Now is the time to pray and cry out for our land and continent, and watch what God will do for us!

Heartcry Ministries
PO Box 737
Oxford
Oxon
OX1 9FA
UK

www.heartcry.co.uk

Other books you may enjoy from Lion Hudson include:

Stepping Stones to Freedom – A 40 day devotional, by Rachel Hickson

Moving in the Prophetic – A biblical guide to effective ministry today, by Greg Haslam

For more information go to
www.lionhudson.com.